The Principles o Ecclesiastical Arc Elucidated by Question and Answer

Matthew Holbeche Bloxam

Alpha Editions

This edition published in 2024

ISBN 9789362515032

Design and Setting By
Alpha Editions
www.alphaedis.com
Email - info@alphaedis.com

Contents

PREFACE.

In revising this Work for a Fourth Edition several alterations have been made, especially in the Concluding Chapter; and the whole has been considerably enlarged.

M. H. B.

Rugby,
April 1841.

Two Arches of Roman Masonry, Leicester.

INTRODUCTION.

ON THE ORIGIN, PROGRESS, AND DECLINE OF GOTHIC OR ENGLISH ECCLESIASTICAL ARCHITECTURE.

AMONGST the vestiges of antiquity which abound in this country, are the visible memorials of those nations which have succeeded one another in the occupancy of this island. To the age of our Celtic ancestors, the earliest possessors of its soil, is ascribed the erection of those altars and temples of all but primeval antiquity, the Cromlechs and Stone Circles which lie scattered over the land; and these are conceived to have been derived from the Phœnicians, whose merchants first introduced amongst the aboriginal Britons the arts of incipient civilization. Of these most ancient relics the prototypes appear, as described in Holy Writ, in the pillar raised at Bethel by Jacob, in the altars erected by the Patriarchs, and in the circles of stone set up by Moses at the foot of Mount Sinai, and by Joshua at Gilgal. Many of these structures, perhaps from their very rudeness, have survived the vicissitudes of time, whilst there scarce remains a vestige of the temples erected in this island by the Romans; yet it is from Roman edifices that we derive, and can trace by a gradual transition, the progress of that peculiar kind of architecture called GOTHIC, which presents in its later stages the most striking contrast that can be imagined to its original precursor.

The Romans having conquered almost the whole of Britain in the first century, retained possession of the southern parts for nearly four hundred years; and during their occupancy they not only instructed the natives in the arts of civilization, but also with their aid, as we learn from Tacitus, began at an early period to erect temples and public edifices, though doubtless much inferior to those at Rome, in their municipal towns and cities. The Christian religion was also early introduced,3-* but for a time its progress was slow; nor was it till the conversion of Constantine, in the fourth century, that it was openly tolerated by the state, and churches were publicly constructed for its worshippers; though even before that event, as we are led to infer from the testimony of Gildas, the most ancient of our native historians, particular structures were appropriated for the performance of its divine mysteries: for that historian alludes to the British Christians as reconstructing the churches which had, in the Dioclesian persecution, been levelled to the ground. But in the fifth century Rome, oppressed on every side by enemies, and distracted with the vastness of her conquests, which she was no longer able to maintain, recalled her legions from Britain; and the Romanized Britons being left without protection, and having, during their subjection to the Romans, lost their ancient valour and love of liberty, in a short time fell a prey to the Northern Barbarians; in their extremity they called over the Saxons to assist them, when the latter perceiving their defenceless condition, turned round upon them, and made an easy conquest of this country. In the struggle which then took place, the churches were again destroyed, the priests were slain at the very altars,4-* and though the British Church was never annihilated, Paganism for a while became triumphant.

Towards the end of the sixth century, when Christianity was again propagated in this country by Augustine, Mellitus, and other zealous monks, St. Gregory, the head of the Papal church, and the originator of this mission, wrote to Mellitus not to suffer the Heathen temples to be destroyed, but only the idols found within them. These, and such churches built by the Romans as were then, though in a dilapidated state, existing, may reasonably be supposed to have been the prototypes of the Christian churches afterwards erected in this country.

In the early period of the empire the Romans imitated the Grecians in their buildings of magnitude and beauty, forming, however, a style of greater richness in detail, though less chaste in effect; and columns of the different orders, with their entablatures, were used to support and adorn their public structures: but in the fourth century, when the arts were declining, the style of architecture became debased, and the predominant features consisted of massive square piers or columns, without entablatures, from the imposts of which sprung arches of a semicircular form; and it was in rude imitation of this latter style that the Saxon churches were constructed.

The Roman basilicas, or halls of justice, some of which were subsequently converted into churches, to which also their names were given, furnished the plan for the internal arrangement of churches of a large size, being divided in the interior by rows of columns. From this division the nave and aisles of a church were derived; and in the semicircular recess at the one end for the tribune, we perceive the origin of the apsis, or semicircular east end, which one of the Anglo-Saxon, and many of our ancient Norman churches still present.

But independent of examples afforded by some few ancient Roman churches, and such of the temples and public buildings of the Romans as were then remaining in Britain, the Saxon converts were directed and assisted in the science of architecture by those missionaries from Rome who propagated Christianity amongst them; and during the Saxon dynasty architects and workmen were frequently procured from abroad, to plan and raise ecclesiastical structures. The Anglo-Saxon churches were, however, rudely built, and, as far as can be ascertained, with some few exceptions, were of no great dimensions and almost entirely devoid of ornamental mouldings, though in some instances decorative sculpture and mouldings are to be met with; but in the repeated incursions of the Danes, in the ninth and tenth centuries, so general was the destruction of the monasteries and churches, which, when the country became tranquil, were rebuilt by the Normans, that we have, in fact, comparatively few churches existing which we may reasonably presume, or really know, to have been erected in an Anglo-Saxon age. Many of the earlier writers on this subject have, however, caused much confusion by applying the term 'SAXON' to all churches and other edifices contradistinguished from the pointed style by semicircular-headed doorways, windows, and arches. But the vestiges of Anglo-Saxon architecture have been as yet so little studied or known, as to render it difficult to point out, either generally or in detail, in what their peculiarities consist: the style may, however, be said to have approximated in appearance much nearer to the Debased Roman style of masonry than the Norman, and to have been also much ruder: and in the most ancient churches, as in that at Dover Castle, and that at Bricksworth, we find arches constructed of flat bricks or tiles, set edgewise, which was also a Roman fashion. The masonry was chiefly composed of rubble, with ashlar or squared blocks of stone at the angles, disposed in courses in a peculiar manner.

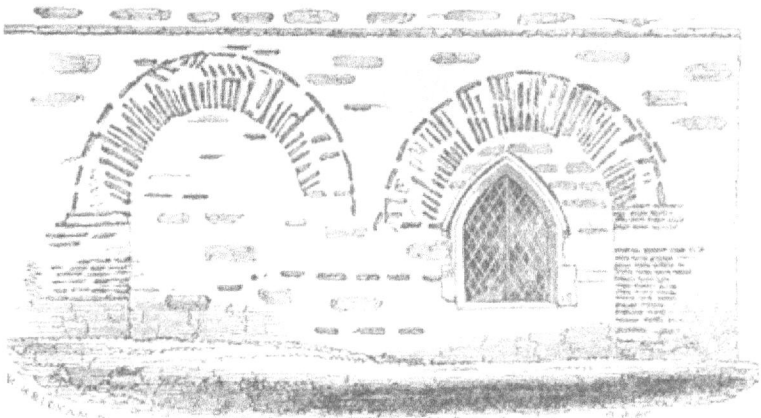

Anglo-Saxon Arches, Bricksworth Church, Northamptonshire (7th. cent.)

The most common characteristic by which the NORMAN style is distinguished, is the semicircular or segmental arch, though this is to be met with also in the rare specimens of Anglo-Saxon masonry; but the Norman arches were more scientifically constructed: in their early state, indeed, quite plain, but generally concentric, or one arch receding within another, and in an advanced stage they were frequently ornamented with zig-zag and other mouldings. A variety of mouldings were also used in the decoration of the Norman portals or doorways, which were besides often enriched with a profusion of sculptured ornament. The Norman churches appear to have much excelled in size the lowly structures of the Saxons, and the cathedral and conventual churches were frequently carried to the height of three tiers or rows of arches, one above another; blank arcades were also used to ornament the walls.

Norman Arcade, St. Aldgate, Oxford.

The Norman style, in which an innumerable number of churches and monastic edifices were originally built or entirely reconstructed, continued without any striking alteration till about the latter part of the twelfth century, when a singular change began to take place: this was no other than the introduction of the pointed arch, the origin of which has never yet been satisfactorily explained, or the precise period clearly ascertained in which it first appeared; but as the lightness and simplicity of design to which the Early Pointed style was found to be afterwards convertible was in its incipient state unknown, it retained to the close of the twelfth century the heavy concomitants of the semicircular arch, with which indeed it was often intermixed: and from such intermixture it may be designated the SEMI or MIXED NORMAN.

When the original Norman style of building was first broken through, by the introduction of the pointed arch, which was often formed by the intersection of semicircular arches, the facing of it, or architrave, was often ornamented with the zig-zag, billet, and other mouldings, in the same manner as the Norman semicircular arches: it also rested on round massive piers, and still retained many other features of Norman architecture. But from the time of its introduction to the close of the twelfth century, the pointed arch was gradually struggling with the semicircular arch for the mastery, and with success; for from the commencement of the thirteenth century, as nearly as can be ascertained, the style of building with semicircular arches was, with very few exceptions, altogether discarded, and superseded by its more elegant rival.

Canterbury Cathedral.

The mode of building with semicircular arches, massive piers, and thick walls with broad pilaster buttresses, was now laid aside; and the pointed arch, supported by more slender piers, with walls strengthened with graduating buttresses, of less width but of greater projection, were universally substituted in their stead. The windows, one of the most apparent marks of distinction, were at first long, narrow, and lancet-shaped: the heavy Norman ornaments, the zig-zag and other mouldings peculiar to the Norman and Semi-Norman styles, were now discarded; yet we often meet with certain decorative ornaments, as the tooth ornament, which, though sometimes found in late Norman work, is almost peculiar to the Early Pointed style; also the ball-flower, prevalent both in this and the style of the succeeding century. Many church towers were also capped with spires, which now first appear. This style prevailed generally throughout the thirteenth century, and is usually designated as the EARLY ENGLISH.

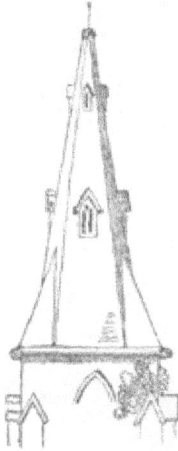

Horsley Ch., Derbyshire.

Towards the close of the thirteenth century a perceptible, though gradual, transition took place to a richer and more ornamental mode of architecture. This was the style of the fourteenth century, and is known by the name of the DECORATED ENGLISH; but it chiefly flourished during the reigns of Edward the Second and Edward the Third, in the latter of which it attained a degree of perfection unequalled by preceding or subsequent ages. Some of the most prominent and distinctive marks of this style occur in the windows, which were greatly enlarged, and divided into many lights by mullions or tracery-bars running into various ramifications above, and dividing the heads into numerous compartments, forming either geometrical or flowing tracery. Triangular or pedimental canopies and pinnacles, more enriched than before with crockets and finials, yet without redundancy of ornament, also occur in the churches built during this century.

Worstead Church, Norfolk.

In the latter part of the fourteenth century another transition, or gradual change of style, began to be effected, in the discrimination of which an obvious distinction again occurs in the composition of the windows, some of which are very large: for the mullion-bars, instead of branching off in the head, in a number of curved lines, are carried up vertically, so as to form *perpendicular* divisions between the window-sill and the head, and do not present that combination of geometrical and flowing tracery observable in the style immediately preceding.

St. Michael's, Oxford.

The frequent occurrence of panelled compartments, and the partial change of form in the arches, especially of doorways and windows, which in the latter part of the fifteenth century were often obtusely pointed and mathematically described from four centres, instead of two, as in the more simple pointed arch, and which from the period when this arch began to be prevalent was called the TUDOR arch, together with a great profusion of minute ornament, mostly of a description not before in use, are the chief characteristics of the style of the fifteenth century, which by some of the earlier writers was designated as the FLORID; though it has since received the more general appellation of the PERPENDICULAR.

This style prevailed till the Reformation, at which period no country could vie with our own in the number of religious edifices, which had been erected in all the varieties of style that had prevailed for many preceding ages. Next to the magnificent cathedrals, the venerable monasteries and collegiate establishments, which had been founded and sumptuously endowed in every part of the kingdom, might most justly claim the preeminence; and many of the churches belonging to them were deservedly held in admiration for their grandeur and architectural elegance of design.

But the suppression of the monasteries tended in no slight degree to hasten the decline and fall of our ancient church architecture, to which other causes, such as the revival of the classic orders in Italy, also contributed. The churches belonging to the conventual foundations, which had been built at different periods by the monks or their benefactors, and the charges of erecting and decorating which from time to time in the most costly manner, had been defrayed out of the monastic revenues, and from private donations, being seized by the crown, were reduced to a state of ruin, and the sites on which they stood granted to dependants of the court. The former reverential feeling on these matters had greatly changed; and as the retention of some few of the ministerial habits, the square cap, the cope, the surplice, and hood, which were deemed expedient for the decent ministration of public worship, gave great offence to many, and was one of the most apparent causes which led to that schism amongst the Reformers, on points of discipline, which afterwards ended in the subversion, for a time, of the rites and ordinances of the Church of England, any attempt towards beautifying and adorning (other than with carved pulpits and communion-tables or altars) the places of divine worship, which were now stripped of many of their former ornamental accessories, would have been regarded and inveighed against as a popish and superstitious innovation; and a charge of this kind was at a later period preferred against Archbishop Laud. Parochial churches were, therefore, now repaired when fallen into a state of dilapidation, in a plain and inelegant mode, in complete variance with the richness and display observable in the style just preceding this event.

Details, originating from the designs of classic architecture, which had been partially revived in Italy, began early in the sixteenth century to make their appearance in this country, though as yet, except on tombs and in wood-work, we observe few of those peculiar features introduced as accessories in church architecture.

Hence many of our country churches, which were repaired or partly rebuilt in the century succeeding the Reformation, exhibit the marks of the style justly denominated DEBASED, to distinguish it from the former purer styles. Depressed and nearly flat arched doorways, with shallow mouldings, square-headed windows with perpendicular mullions and obtuse-pointed or round-headed lights, without foliations, together with a general clumsiness of construction, as compared with more ancient edifices, form the predominating features in ecclesiastical buildings of this kind: and in the reign of Charles the First an indiscriminate mixture of Debased Gothic and Roman architecture prevailing, we lose sight of every true feature of our ancient ecclesiastical styles, which were superseded by that which sprang more immediately from the Antique, the Roman, or Italian mode.

3-* Tempore, ut scimus, summo Tiberii Cæsaris, &c.—GILDAS.

4-* Ruebant ædificia publica simul et privata, passim Sacerdotes inter altaria trucibantur.—BEDE, Eccl. Hist. lib. i. c. xv.

Scutcheon from Beauchamp Chapel, Warwick, circa A. D. 1450.

CHAPTER I.

DEFINITION OF GOTHIC ARCHITECTURE; ITS ORIGIN, AND THE DIVISION OF IT INTO STYLES.

Q. WHAT is meant by the term "Gothic Architecture"?

A. Without entering into the derivation of the word "Gothic," it may suffice to state that it is an expression sometimes used to denote in one general term, and distinguish from the Antique, those peculiar modes or styles in which most of our ecclesiastical and many of our domestic edifices of the middle ages have been built. In a more confined sense, it comprehends those styles only in which the pointed arch predominates, and it is then often used to distinguish such from the more ancient Anglo-Saxon and Norman styles.

Q. To what can the origin of this kind of architecture be traced?

A. To the classic orders in that state of degeneracy into which they had fallen in the age of Constantine, and afterwards; and as the Romans, on their voluntary abandonment of Britain in the fifth century, left many of their temples and public edifices remaining, together with some Christian churches, it was in rude imitation of the Roman structures of the fourth century that the most ancient of our Anglo-Saxon churches were constructed. This is apparent from an examination and comparison of such with the vestiges of Roman buildings we have existing.

Q. Into how many different styles may English ecclesiastical architecture be divided?

A. No specific regulation has been adopted, with regard to the denomination or division of the several styles, in which all the writers on the subject agree: but they may be divided into seven, which, together with the periods when they flourished, may be generally defined as follows:

The SAXON Or ANGLO-SAXON Style, which prevailed from the mission of Augustine, at the close of the sixth, to the middle of the eleventh century.

The NORMAN style, which may be said to have prevailed generally from the middle of the eleventh to the latter part of the twelfth century.

The SEMI-NORMAN, Or TRANSITION style, which appears to have prevailed during the latter part of the twelfth century.

The EARLY ENGLISH, or general style of the thirteenth century.

The DECORATED ENGLISH, or general style of the fourteenth century.

The FLORID Or PERPENDICULAR ENGLISH, the style of the fifteenth, and early part of the sixteenth century.

The DEBASED ENGLISH, or general style of the latter part of the sixteenth and early part of the seventeenth century, towards the middle of which Gothic architecture, even in its debased state, became entirely discarded.

Q. What constitutes the difference of these styles?

A. They may be distinguished partly by the form of the arches, which are triangular-headed, semicircular or segmental, simple pointed, and complex pointed; though such forms are by no means an invariable criterion of any particular style; by the size and shape of the windows, and the manner in which they are subdivided or not by transoms, mullions, and tracery; but more especially by certain minute details, ornamental accessories and mouldings, more or less peculiar to particular styles, and which are seldom to be met with in any other.

Q. Are the majority of our ecclesiastical buildings composed only of one style?

A. Most of our cathedral and country churches have been built, or had additions made to them, at different periods, and therefore seldom exhibit an uniformity of design; and many churches have details about them of almost every style. There are, however, numerous exceptions, where churches have been erected in the same style throughout; and this is more particularly observable in the churches of the fifteenth century.

Q. Were they constructed on any regular plan?

A. The general ground plan of cathedral and conventual churches was after the form of a cross, and the edifice consisted of a central tower, with transepts running north and south; westward of the tower was the nave or main body of the structure, with lateral aisles; and the west front contained the principal entrance, and was often flanked by towers. Eastward of the central tower was the choir, where the principal service was performed, with aisles on each side, and beyond this was the lady chapel. Sometimes the design also comprehended other chapels. On the north or south side was the chapter house, in early times quadrangular, but afterwards octagonal in plan; and on the same side, in most instances, though not always, were the cloisters, which communicated immediately with the church, and surrounded a quadrangular court. The chapter house and cloisters we still find remaining as adjuncts to most cathedral churches, though the conventual buildings of a domestic nature, with which the cloisters formerly also communicated, have generally been destroyed. Mere parochial churches have commonly a tower at the west end, a nave with lateral aisles, and a chancel. Some churches have transepts; and small side chapels or additional aisles have been annexed to many, erected at the costs of individuals, to serve for burial and as chantries. The smallest class of churches have a nave and chancel only, with a small bell-turret formed of wooden shingles, or an open arch of stonework, appearing above the roof at the west end.

St. Martin's, Leicester, circa A. D. 1250.

CHAPTER II.

OF THE DIFFERENT KINDS OF ARCHES.

Q. DO the distinctions of the different styles, as they differ from each other, depend at all upon the form of the arch?

A. To a certain extent the form of the arch may be considered as a criterion of style; too much dependence, however, must not be placed on this rule, inasmuch as there are many exceptions.

Q. How are arches divided generally, as to form?

A. Into the triangular-headed or straight-lined pointed arch, the round-headed arch, and the curved-pointed arch; and the latter are again subdivided.

Q. How is the triangular-headed or straight-lined pointed arch formed, and when did it prevail?

A. It may be described as formed by the two upper sides of a triangle, more or less obtuse or acute. It is generally considered as one of the characteristics of the Anglo-Saxon style, where it is often to be met with of plain and rude construction. But instances of this form of arch, though they are not frequent, are to be met with in the Norman and subsequent styles. Arches, however, of this description, of late date, may be generally known by some moulding or other feature peculiar to the style in which it is used.

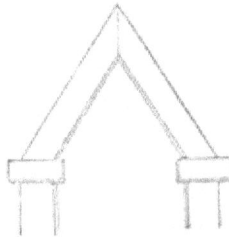

Q. What different kinds of round-headed arches are there?

A. The semicircular arch (fig. 1), the stilted arch (fig. 2), the segmental arch (fig. 3), and the horse-shoe arch (fig. 4).

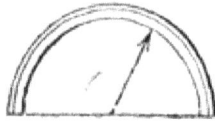

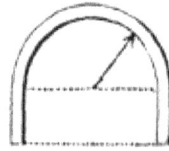

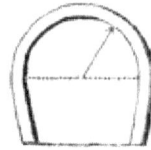

Q. How are they formed or described?

A. The semicircular arch is described from a centre in the same line with its spring; the stilted arch in the same manner, but the sides are carried downwards in a straight line below the spring of the curve till they rest upon the imposts; the segmental arch is described from a centre lower than its spring; and the horse-shoe arch from a centre placed above its spring.

Q. During what period of time do we find these arches generally in use?

A. The semicircular arch, which is the most common, we find to have prevailed from the time of the Romans to the close of the twelfth century, when it became generally discarded; and we seldom meet with it again, in its simple state, till about the middle of the sixteenth century. It is in some degree considered as a characteristic of the Anglo-Saxon and Norman styles. The stilted arch is chiefly found in conjunction with the semicircular arch in the construction of Norman vaulting over a space in plan that of a parallelogram. The segmental arch we meet with in almost all the styles, used as an arch of construction, and for doorway and window arches; whilst the form of the horse-shoe arch seems, in many instances, to have been occasioned by the settlement and inclination of the piers from which it springs.

Q. Into how many classes may the pointed arch be divided?

A. Into two, namely, the simple pointed arch described from two centres, and the complex pointed arch described from four centres.

Q. What are the different kinds of simple pointed arches?

A. The LANCET, or acute-pointed arch; the EQUILATERAL pointed arch; and the OBTUSE-ANGLED pointed arch.

Q. How is the lancet arch formed and described?

A. It is formed of two segments of a circle, and its centres have a radius or line longer than the breadth of the arch, and may be described from an acute-angled triangle. (fig. 5.).

Q. How is the equilateral arch formed and described?

A. From two segments of a circle; the centres of it have a radius or line equal to the breadth of the arch, and it may be described from an equilateral triangle. (fig. 6.)

5.   6.   7.

Q. How is the obtuse-angled arch formed and described?

A. Like the foregoing, it is formed from two segments of a circle, and the centres of it have a radius shorter than the breadth of the arch; it is described from an obtuse-angled triangle. (fig. 7.)

Q. During what period were these pointed arches in use?

A. They were all gradually introduced in the twelfth century, and continued during the thirteenth century; after which the lancet arch appears to have been generally discarded, though the other two prevailed till a much later period.

Q. What are the different kinds of complex pointed arches?

A. Those commonly called the OGEE, or contrasted arch; and the TUDOR arch.

Q. How is the ogee, or contrasted arch, formed and described?

A. It is formed of four segments of a circle, and is described from four centres, two placed within the arch on a level with the spring, and two placed on the exterior of the arch, and level with the apex or point (fig. 8); each side is composed of a double curve, the lowermost convex and the uppermost concave.

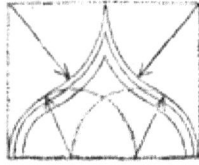

S.

9.

Q. When was the ogee arch introduced, and how long did it prevail?

A. It was introduced early in the fourteenth century, and continued till the close of the fifteenth century.

Q. How is the Tudor arch described?

A. From four centres; two on a level with the spring, and two at a distance from it, and below. (fig. 9.)

Q. When was the Tudor arch introduced, and why is it so called?

A. It was introduced about the middle of the fifteenth century, or perhaps earlier, but became most prevalent during the reigns of Henry the Seventh and Henry the Eighth, under the Tudor dynasty, from which it derives its name.

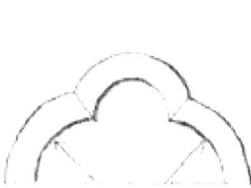

10.

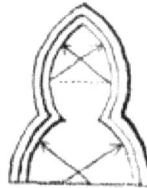

11.

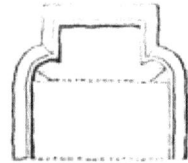

12.

Q. What other kinds of arches are there worthy of notice?

A. Those which are called foiled arches, as the round-headed trefoil (fig. 10), the pointed trefoil (fig. 11), and the square-headed trefoil (fig. 12). The first prevailed in the latter part of the twelfth and early part of the thirteenth century, chiefly as a heading for niches or blank arcades; the second, used for the same purpose, we find to have prevailed in the thirteenth century; and the latter is found in doorways of the thirteenth, fourteenth, and fifteenth centuries. In all these the exterior mouldings follow the same curvatures as the inner mouldings, and are thus distinguishable from arches the heads of which are only foliated within.

St. Thomas's, Oxford, circa 1250.

Anglo-Saxon Doorway, Brixworth Church, Northamptonshire. (7th cent.)

CHAPTER III.

OF THE ANGLO-SAXON STYLE.

Q. DURING what period of time did this style prevail?

A. From the close of the sixth century, when the conversion of the Anglo-Saxons commenced, to the middle of the eleventh century.

Q. Whence does this style appear to have derived its origin?

A. From the later Roman edifices; for in the most ancient of the Anglo-Saxon remains we find an approximation, more or less, to the Roman mode of building, with arches formed of brickwork.

Q. What is peculiar in the constructive features of Roman masonry?

A. Walls of Roman masonry in this country were chiefly constructed of stone or flint, according to the part of the country in which the one material or other prevailed, embedded in mortar, bonded at certain intervals throughout with regular horizontal courses or layers of large flat Roman bricks or tiles, which, from the inequality of thickness and size, do not appear to have been shaped in any regular mould.

Portion of the Fragment of a Roman Building at Leicester.

Q. What vestiges of Roman masonry are now existing in Britain?

A. A fragment, apparently that of a Roman temple or basilica, near the church of St. Nicholas at Leicester, which contains horizontal courses of brick at intervals, and arches constructed of brickwork; the curious portion of a wall of similar construction, with remains of brick arches on the one side, which indicate it to have formed part of a building, and not a mere wall as it now appears, at Wroxeter, Salop; and the polygonal tower at Dover Castle, which, notwithstanding an exterior casing of flint, and other alterations effected in the fifteenth century, still retains many visible features of its original construction of tufa bonded with bricks at intervals. Roman masonry, of the mixed description of brick and stone, regularly disposed, is found in walls at York, Lincoln, Silchester, and elsewhere; and sometimes we meet with bricks or stone arranged herring-bone fashion, as in the vestiges of a Roman building at Castor, Northamptonshire, and the walls of a Roman villa discovered at Littleton, Somersetshire.

Q. Have we any remains of the ancient British churches erected in this country in the third, fourth, or fifth centuries?

A. None such have yet been discovered or noticed; for the ruinous structure at Perranzabuloe in Cornwall, which some assert to have been an ancient British church, is probably not of earlier date than the twelfth century; and the church of St. Martin at Canterbury, built in the time of the Romans, which Augustine found on his arrival still used for the worship of God, was rebuilt in the thirteenth century, but, to all appearance, with the same materials of which the original church was constructed.

Q. Do any of our churches bear a resemblance to Roman buildings?

A. The church now in ruins within the precincts of the Castle of Dover presents features of early work approximating Roman, as a portal and window-arches formed of brickwork, which seem to have been copied from those in the Roman tower near adjoining; the walls also have much of Roman brick worked up into them, but have no such regular horizontal layers as Roman masonry displays. The most ancient portions of this church are attributed to belong to the middle of the seventh century. The church of Brixworth, Northamptonshire, is perhaps the most complete specimen we have existing of an early Anglo-Saxon church: it has had side aisles separated from the nave by semicircular arches constructed of Roman bricks, with wide joints; these arches spring from square and plain massive piers. There is also fair recorded evidence to support the inference that this church is a structure of the latter part of the seventh century. Roman bricks are worked up in the walls, in no regular order, however, but indiscriminately, as in the church at Dover Castle.

Pilaster Rib-work Arch, Brigstock Church.

Q. What peculiarities are observable in masonry of Anglo-Saxon construction?

A. From existing vestiges of churches of presumed Anglo-Saxon construction it appears that the walls were chiefly formed of rubble or rag-stone, covered on the exterior with stucco or plaster, with long and short blocks of ashlar or hewn stone, disposed at the angles in alternate courses. We also find, projecting a few inches from the surface of the wall, and running up vertically, narrow ribs or square-edged strips of stone, bearing from their position a rude similarity to pilasters; and these strips are generally composed of long and short pieces of stone placed alternately. A plain string course of the same description of square-edged rib or strip-work often runs horizontally along the walls of Anglo-Saxon remains, and the vertical ribs are sometimes set upon such as a basement, and sometimes finish under such.

Q. What churches exhibit projecting strips of stonework thus disposed?

A. The towers of the churches of Earls Barton and Barnack, Northamptonshire, and the tower of one of the churches at Barton-upon-Humber, Lincolnshire, are covered with these narrow projecting strips of stonework, in such a manner that the surface of the wall appears divided into rudely formed panels; the like disposition of rib-work appears, though not to so great extent, on the face of the upper part of the tower of Stowe Church, Northamptonshire, of St. Benedict's Church, Cambridge, on the walls of the church of Worth, in Sussex, on the upper part of the walls of the chancel of Repton Church, Derbyshire, and on the walls of the nave and north transept of Stanton Lacey Church, Salop.

Anglo-Saxon Masonry, Long and Short Work.

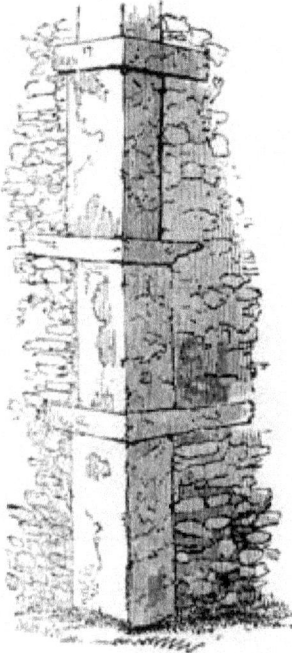

Burcombe, Wilts.   Wittering, Northamptonshire.

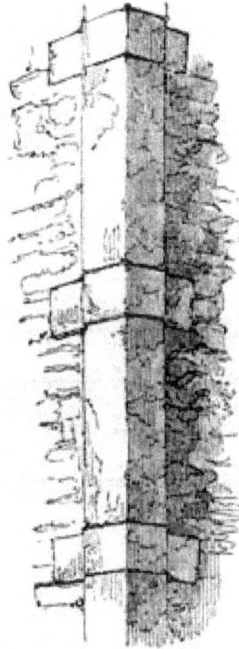

Q. Where do we meet with instances where long and short blocks of ashlar masonry are disposed in alternate courses at the angles of walls?

A. Such occur at the angles of the chancel of North Burcombe Church, Wiltshire; at the angles of the nave and chancel of Wittering Church, Northamptonshire; at the angles of the towers of St. Benedict's Church, Cambridge, of Sompting Church, Sussex, and of St. Michael's Church, Oxford, and in other Anglo-Saxon remains. The ashlar masonry forming the angles is not, however, invariably thus disposed.

Q. How are the doorways of this style distinguished?

A. They are either semicircular, or triangular-arched headed, but the former are more common. In those, apparently the most ancient, the voussoirs or arched heads are faced with large flat bricks or tiles, closely resembling Roman work. Doorways of this description are to be met with in the old church, Dover Castle; in the church of Brixworth, Northamptonshire; and on the south side of Brytford Church, Wiltshire. The doorway, however, we most frequently meet with in Anglo-Saxon remains, is of simple yet peculiar construction, semicircular-headed, and formed entirely of stone, without any admixture of brick; the jambs are square-edged, and are sometimes but not always composed of two long blocks placed upright, with a short block between them; the arched head of the doorway is plain, and springs from square projecting impost blocks, the under edges of which are sometimes bevelled and sometimes left square. This doorway is contained within a kind of arch of rib-work, projecting from the face of the wall, with strips of pilaster rib-work continued down to the ground; sometimes this arch springs from plain block imposts, or from strips of square-edged rib-work disposed horizontally, and the jambs are occasionally constructed of long and short work.

Anglo-Saxon Doorway, St. Peter's Church, Barton-upon-Humber.

Q. Mention the names of churches in which doorways of this description are preserved?

A. The south doorways of the towers of the old church at Barton-upon-Humber and of Barnack Church, the west doorway of the tower of

Earls Barton Church, the north and south doorways of the tower of Wooten Wawen Church, Warwickshire, the east doorway of the tower of Stowe Church, Northamptonshire, the north doorway of the nave of Brytford Church, Wiltshire, and the north doorway of the nave of Stanton Lacey Church, Salop, though differing in some respects from each other, bear a general similarity of design, and come under the foregoing description.

Belfry Window, north side of the Tower of Wyckham Church, Berks.

Q. How are we able to distinguish the windows of the Anglo-Saxon style?

A. The belfry windows are generally found to consist of two semicircular-headed lights, divided by a kind of rude balluster shaft of peculiar character, the entasis of which is sometimes encircled with rude annulated mouldings; this shaft supports a plain oblong impost or abacus, which extends through the whole of the thickness of the wall, or nearly so, and from this one side of the arch of each light springs. Double windows thus divided appear in the belfry stories of the church towers of St. Michael, Oxford; St. Benedict, Cambridge; St. Peter, Barton-upon-Humber; Wyckham, Berks; Sompting, Sussex; and Northleigh, Oxfordshire. In the belfry of the tower of Earls Barton Church are windows of five or six lights, the divisions between which are formed by these curious balluster shafts. The semicircular-headed single-light window of this style may be distinguished from those of the Norman style by the double splay of the jambs, the spaces between which spread or increase in width outwardly as well as inwardly, the narrowest part of the window being placed on the centre of the thickness of the wall; whereas the jambs of windows in the

Norman style have only a single splay, and the narrowest part of the window is set even with the external face of the wall, or nearly so. Single-light windows splayed externally occur in the west walls of the towers of Wyckham Church, Berks, and of Stowe Church, Northamptonshire, Caversfield Church, Oxfordshire, and on the north side of the chancel of Clapham Church, Bedfordshire; but windows without a splay occur in the tower of Lavendon Church, Buckinghamshire. Small square or oblong-shaped apertures are sometimes met with, as in the tower of St. Benedict's Church, Cambridge; and also triangular-headed windows, which, with doorways of the same form, will be presently noticed.

Anglo-Saxon Single-light Window, Tower of Wyckham Church, Berks.

Q. Of what description are the arches which separate the nave from the chancel and aisles, and sustain the clerestory walls?

Anglo-Saxon Arches, St. Michael's Church, St. Alban's, A. D. 948.

A. They are very plain, and consist of a single sweep or soffit only, without any sub-arch, as in the Norman style; and they spring from square piers; with a plain abacus impost on each intervening, which impost has sometimes the under edge chamfered, and sometimes left quite plain. Arches of this description occur at Brixworth Church, between the nave and chancel of Clapham Church, and between the nave and chancel of Wyckham Church. The arches in St. Michael's Church, St. Alban's, which divide the nave from the aisles, have their edges slightly chamfered. There are also arches with single soffits, which have over them a kind of hood, similar to that over doorways of square-edged rib-work, projecting a few inches from the face of the wall, carried round the arch, and either dying into the impost or continued straight down to the ground. The chancel arch of Worth Church, and arches in the churches of Brigstock and Barnack, and of St. Benedict, Cambridge, and the chancel arch, Barrow Church, Salop, are of this description. Some arches have round or semicylindrical mouldings rudely worked on the face, as in the chancel arch, Wittering Church; or under or attached to the soffit, as at the churches of Sompting and St. Botulph, Sussex. Rudely sculptured impost blocks also sometimes occur, as at Sompting and at St. Botulph; and animals sculptured in low relief appear at the springing of the hood over the arch in the tower of St. Benedict's Church, Cambridge.

Tower Arch, Barnack Church, Northamptonshire.

Chancel Arch, Wittering Church, Northamptonshire.

Q. How are some of the doorways, windows, arched recesses, and panels of Anglo-Saxon architecture constructed?

Doorway in the Tower of Brigstock Church.

A. In a very rude manner, of two or more long blocks of stone, placed slantingly or inclined one towards the other, thus forming a straight line, or triangular-headed arch; the lower ends of these sometimes rest on plain projecting imposts, which surmount other blocks composing the jambs. We find a doorway of this description on the west side of the tower of Brigstock Church, forming the entrance into the curious circular-shaped turret attached and designed for a staircase to the belfry; an arched recess of this description occurs in the tower of Barnack Church, and a panel on the exterior of the same tower, and in windows in the tower of the old church, Barton-upon-Humber, and in the tower of Sompting Church, and St. Michael's Church, Oxford. The arch thus shaped is not, however, peculiar to the Anglo-Saxon style, but may occasionally be traced in most if not all of the subsequent styles, but not of such rude or plain construction.

Recess in the Tower of Barnack Church.

Q. Were the Anglo-Saxon architects accustomed to construct crypts beneath their churches?

A. There are some subterranean vaults, not easily accessible, the presumed remains of Bishop Wilfrid's work, at Ripon and Hexham, of the latter part of the seventh century; but the crypt beneath the chancel of Repton Church, Derbyshire, the walls of which are constructed of *hewn* stone, is perhaps the most perfect specimen existing of a crypt in the Anglo-Saxon style, and of a stone vaulted roof sustained by piers, which are of singular character; the vaulting is without diagonal groins, and bears a greater similarity to Roman than to Norman vaulting.

Crypt, Repton Church, Derbyshire.

Q. Are mouldings, or is any kind of sculptured ornament, to be met with in Anglo-Saxon work?

A. Although the remains of this style are for the most part plain and devoid of ornamental detail, we occasionally meet with mouldings of a semicylindrical or roll-like form, on the face or under the soffit of an arch, and these are sometimes continued down the sides of the jambs or piers. Foliage, knot-work, and other rudely sculptured detail occur on the tower of Barnack Church, and some rude sculptures appear in St. Benedict's Church, Cambridge; and the plain and simple cross of the Greek form, is represented in relief over a doorway at Stanton Lacey Church, and over windows in the tower of Earls Barton Church.

Q. What was the general plan of the Anglo-Saxon churches?

A. We have now but few instances in which the complete ground plan of an Anglo-Saxon church can be traced: that of Worth Church, Sussex, is perhaps the most perfect, as the original foundation walls do not appear to have been disturbed, although insertions of windows of later date have been made in the walls of the superstructure. This church is planned in the form of a cross, and consists of a nave with transepts, and a chancel, terminating at the east end with a semicircular apsis—a rare instance in the Anglo-Saxon style, as in general the east end of the chancel is rectangular in plan. The towers of Anglo-Saxon churches are generally placed at the west end, though sometimes, as at Wotten Wawen, they occur between the chancel and nave. No original staircase has yet been found in the interior of any. The church at Brixworth, an edifice of the seventh century, and that of St. Michael, at St. Alban's, of the tenth century, have aisles. Sometimes the church appears to have consisted of a nave and chancel only.

Q. Why have we so few ecclesiastical remains of known or presumed Anglo-Saxon architecture now existing?

A. There are probably many examples of this style preserved in churches which have hitherto escaped observation49-*; still they are, comparatively speaking, rarely to be met with: and this may be accounted for by the recorded fact, that in the repeated incursions of the Danes in this island, during the ninth and tenth centuries, almost all the Anglo-Saxon monasteries and churches were set on fire and destroyed.

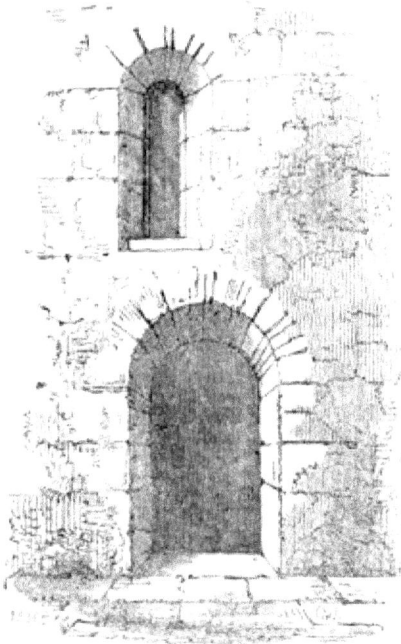

Anglo Saxon Doorway and Window, interior of the tower of Brigstock Church, north side.

49-* All the Anglo-Saxon remains noticed in this chapter, except those alluded to as supposed to exist at Ripon and Hexham, together with the tower of the church of St. Benedict's, Lincoln, have been inspected by the author; and the illustrations of this chapter are, with three exceptions, from his sketches made on the spot. Of the remaining three vignettes, two are from drawings made whilst the author was present, and one only, viz.

that of the crypt beneath the chancel of Repton Church, has been reduced from a larger engraving. Besides the churches which have been referred to, several others which have not been visited by the author exhibit vestiges, more or less, of presumed Anglo-Saxon work. Of such churches the following is a list, and, with those mentioned in the chapter, constitute all which have yet come under his notice:

- Caversfield, Oxfordshire.
- Church Stretton, Salop.
- Trinity Church, Colchester.
- Deerhurst, Gloucestershire.
- Daglinworth, Gloucestershire.
- Jarrow, Durham.
- Laughton-en-le-Morthen, Yorkshire.
- Kirkdale, Yorkshire.
- Monkswearmouth, Durham.
- Ropsley, Lincolnshire.
- Stoke D'Abernon, Surrey.
- Wittingham, Yorkshire.

Of these, seven are noticed by Mr. Rickman.

Norman Chancel, Darent Church, Kent.

CHAPTER IV.

OF THE NORMAN OR ANGLO-NORMAN STYLE.

Q. TO what era may we assign the introduction of the Anglo-Norman style?

A. To the reign of Edward the Confessor, since that monarch is recorded by the historians, Matthew Paris and William of Malmesbury, to have rebuilt (A. D. 1065) the Abbey Church at Westminster in a new style of architectural design, which furnished an example afterwards followed by many in the construction of churches.52-*

Q. Is any portion of the structure erected by Edward the Confessor remaining?

A. A crypt of early Norman work under the present edifice or buildings attached to it is supposed to have been part of the church constructed by that monarch.

Q. During what period of time did this style prevail?

A. From about A. D. 1065 to the close of the twelfth century.

Q. By what means are we to distinguish this style from the styles of a later period?

A. It is distinguished without difficulty by its semicircular arches, its massive piers, which are generally square or cylindrical, though sometimes multangular in form, and from numerous ornamental details and mouldings peculiar to the style.

Q. What part of the original building has generally been preserved in those churches that were built by the Normans, when all the rest has been demolished and rebuilt in a later style of architecture?

Norman Doorway, Wolston Church, Warwickshire.

A. There appears to have been a prevalent custom, among those architects who succeeded the Normans, to preserve the doorways of those churches they rebuilt or altered; for many such doorways still remain in churches, the other portions of which were built at a much later period. Thus in the tower of Kenilworth Church, Warwickshire, is a Norman doorway of singular design, from the square band or ornamental facia which environs it. This is a relic of a more ancient edifice than the structure in which it now appears, and which is of the fourteenth century; and the external masonry of the doorway is not tied into the walls of more recent construction, but exhibits a break all round. The church of Stoneleigh, in the same county, contains in the north wall a fine Norman doorway, which has been left undisturbed, though the wall on each side of Norman construction, has been altered, not by demolition, but by the insertion, in the fourteenth century, of decorated windows in lieu of the original small Norman lights.

Q. Were the Norman doorways much ornamented?

A. Many rich doorways were composed of a succession of receding semicircular arches springing from rectangular-edged jambs, and detached shafts with capitals in the nooks; which shafts, together with the arches, were often enriched with the mouldings common to this style. Sometimes the sweep of mouldings which faced the architrave was continued without intermission down the jambs or sides of the doorway; and in small country churches Norman doorways, quite plain in their construction, or with but few mouldings, are to be met with. There is, perhaps, a greater variety of design in doorways of this than of any other style; and of the numerous mouldings with which they in general abound more or less, the chevron, or zig-zag, appears to have been the most common.

Q. In what other respect were these doors sometimes ornamented?

A. The semicircular-shaped stone, which we often find in the tympanum at the back of the head of the arch, is generally covered with rude sculpture in basso relievo, sometimes representing a scriptural subject, as the temptation of our first parents on the tympanum of a Norman doorway at Thurley Church, Bedfordshire; sometimes a legend, as a curious and very early sculpture over the south door of Fordington Church, Dorsetshire, representing a scene in the story of St. George; and sometimes symbolical, as the representation of fish, serpents, and chimeræ on the north doorway of Stoneleigh Church, Warwickshire. The figure of our Saviour in a sitting attitude, holding in his left hand a book, and with his right arm and hand upheld, in allusion to the saying, *I am the way, and the truth, and the life*, and circumscribed by that mystical figure the *Vesica piscis*, appears over Norman doorways at Ely Cathedral; Rochester Cathedral; Malmesbury Abbey Church; Elstow Church, Bedfordshire; Water Stratford Church, Buckinghamshire; and Barfreston Church, Kent; and is not uncommon.

Q. Are there many Norman porches?

A. Norman porches occur at Durham Cathedral; Malmesbury Abbey Church; Sherbourne Abbey Church; and Witney Church, Oxfordshire; but they are not very common. The roof of the porch was usually groined with simple cross springers and moulded ribs; and in some instances a room over has been added at a later period. Numerous portals of the Norman era appear constructed within a shallow projecting mass of masonry, similar in appearance to the broad projecting buttress, and, like that, finished on the upper edge with a plain slope. This was to give a sufficiency of depth to the numerous concentric arches successively receding in the thickness of the wall, which could not otherwise be well attained.

Q. What kind of windows were those belonging to this style?

A. The windows were mostly small and narrow, seldom of more than one light, except belfry windows, which were usually divided into two round-headed lights by a shaft, with a capital and abacus. Early in the style the windows were quite plain; afterwards they were ornamented in a greater or less degree, sometimes with the chevron or zig-zag, and sometimes with roll or cylinder mouldings; in many instances, also, shafts were inserted at the sides, the window jambs were simply splayed in one direction only, and the space between them increased in width inwardly.

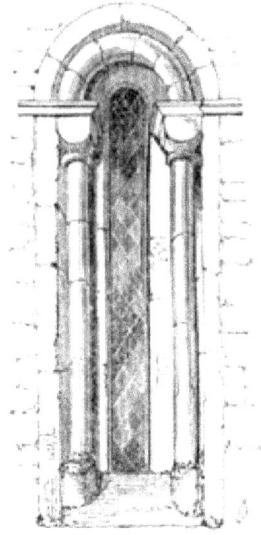

Norman Window, Ryton Church, Warwickshire.

Q. Do we meet with any circular or wheel-shaped windows of the Norman era?

A. A circular window, with divisions formed by small shafts and semicircular or trefoiled arches, disposed so as to converge to a common centre, sometimes occurs in the gable at the east end of a Norman church, as at Barfreston Church, Kent; and New Shoreham Church, Sussex; and are not uncommon.

Early Norman Window, Darent Church, Kent, with incipient zig-zag moulding.

Q. What kinds of piers were the Norman piers?

A. Early in the style they were (with some exceptions, as in the crypts beneath the cathedrals of Canterbury and Worcester) very massive, and the generality plain and cylindrical; though sometimes they were square, which was indeed the most ancient shape; sometimes they appear with rectangular nooks or recesses; and, in large churches, Norman piers had frequently one or more semicylindrical pier-shafts attached, disposed either in nooks or on the face of the pier. We sometimes meet with octagonal piers, as in the cathedrals of Oxford and Peterborough, the conventual church at Ely, and in the ruined church of Buildwas Abbey, Salop; and also, though rarely, with piers covered with spiral flutings, as one is in Norwich Cathedral; with the spiral cable moulding, as one is in the crypt of Canterbury Cathedral; and encircled with a spiral band, as one appears in the ruined chapel at Orford, in Suffolk; sometimes, also, they appear covered with ornamental mouldings. Late in the style the piers assume a greater lightness in appearance, and are sometimes clustered and banded round with mouldings, and approximate in design those of a subsequent style.

Q. How are the capitals distinguished?

A. The general outline and shape of the Norman capital is that of a square cubical mass, having the lower part rounded off with a contour resembling that of an ovolo moulding; the face on each side of the upper part of the capital is flat, and it is often separated from the lower part by an escalloped edge; and where such division is formed by more than one escallop, the lower part is channelled between each, and the spaces below the escalloped edges are worked or moulded so as to resemble inverted and truncated semicones.

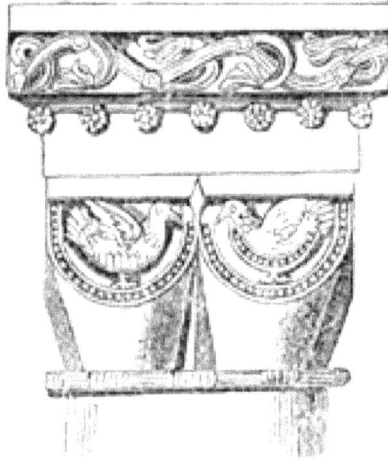

Norman Capital, Steetley Church, Derbyshire.

Besides the plain capital thus described, of which instances with the single escalloped edge occur in the crypts beneath the cathedrals of Canterbury, Winchester, and Worcester, and with a series of escalloped edges, or what would be heraldically termed *invected*, in many of the capitals of the Norman piers in Norwich Cathedral, an extreme variety of design in ornamental accessories prevail, the general form and outline of the capital being preserved; and some exhibit imitations of the Ionic volute and Corinthian acanthus, whilst many are covered with rude sculpture in relief. They are generally finished with a plain square abacus moulding, with the under edge simply bevelled or chamfered; sometimes a slight angular moulding occurs between the upper face and slope of the abacus, and sometimes the abacus alone intervenes between the pier and the spring of the arch. There are also many round capitals, as, for instance, those in the nave of Gloucester Cathedral, but they are mostly late in the style.

Norman Arcade, St. Augustine's, Canterbury.

Q. What is observable in the bases of the piers?

A. The common base moulding resembles in form or contour a quirked ovolo reversed; there are, however, many exceptions.

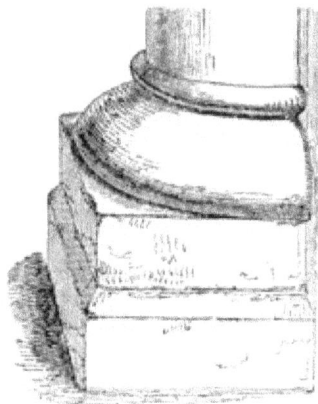

Norman Base, Romsey Church, Hants.

Q. How are the arches distinguished?

A. By their semicircular form; they are generally double-faced, or formed of two concentric divisions, one receding within the other. Early in the style they are plain and square-edged; late in the style they are often found enriched with the zig-zag and roll mouldings, or some other ornament. Sometimes the curvature of the arch does not immediately spring from the capital or impost, but is raised or stilted.

Q. What parts of Norman churches do we generally find vaulted?

A. In cathedral and large conventual churches built in the Norman style we find the crypts and aisles vaulted with stone, but not the nave or choir; and over the vaulting of the aisles was the triforium. In small Norman churches the chancel is generally the only part vaulted; and between the vaulting and outer roof is, in some instances, a small loft or chamber. Sometimes we find the original design for vaulting to have been commenced and left unfinished.

Norman Arch and Piers, Melbourne Church, Derbyshire.

Q. Of what description was the Norman vaulting?

A. The bays of vaulting were generally either squares or parallelograms, though sometimes not rectangular in shape, and each was divided into four concave vaulting cells by diagonal and intersecting groins, thus forming what is called a quadripartite vault. Early in the style the diagonal edges of the groins appear without ribs or mouldings; at an advanced stage they are supported by square-edged ribs of cut stone; and late in the style the ribs and groins are faced with roll or cylinder mouldings. They are also sometimes profusely covered with the zig-zag moulding and other ornamental details.

Q. What is observable with respect to Norman masonry?

A. In general the walls are faced on each side with a thin shell of ashlar or cut stone, whilst the intervening space, which is sometimes considerable, is filled with grouted rubble. Masses of this grout-work masonry, from which the facing of cut stone has been removed, we often find amongst ruined edifices of early date.

Q. Were there any buttresses used at this period?

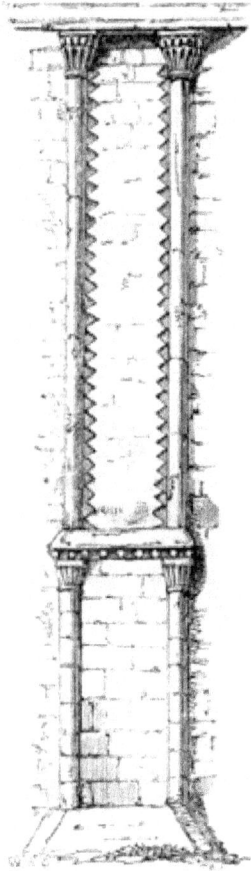

Norman Buttress, Chancel of St. Mary's, Leicester.

A. Yes; but the walls being enormously thick, and requiring little additional support, those in use are like pilasters, with a broad face projecting very little from the building; and they seem to have been derived from the pilaster strips of stonework in Anglo-Saxon masonry. They are generally of a single stage only, but sometimes of more, and are not carried up higher than the cornice, under which they often but not always finish with a slope. They appear as if intended rather to relieve the plain external surface of the wall than to strengthen it. Norman portals not unfrequently occur, formed in the thickness of a broad but shallow pilaster buttress, as at

Iffley Church, Oxfordshire, and at Stoneleigh and Hampton-in-Arden Churches, Warwickshire, and elsewhere. This kind of buttress was also used in the next, or Semi-Norman style.

Q. Were there any towers?

A. Yes; they were generally very low and massive; and the exterior, especially of the upper story, was often decorated with arcades of blank semicircular and intersecting arches; the parapet consisted of a plain projecting blocking-course, supported by the corbel table.

Q. Do pinnacles appear to have been known to the Normans?

A. Although some are of opinion that the pinnacle was not introduced till after the adoption of the pointed style, many Norman buildings have pinnacles of a conical shape, which are apparently part of the original design.

Q. What distinction occurs in the construction of the small country churches of this style, and the larger buildings of conventual foundation?

A. Small Norman churches consisted of a single story only; cathedral and conventual churches were carried up to a great height, and were frequently divided into three tiers, the lowest of which consisted of single arches, separating the nave from the aisles: above each of these arches in the second tier were two smaller arches constructed beneath a larger; sometimes the same space was occupied by a single arch; and in this tier was the triforium or gallery. In the third tier or clerestory were frequently arcades of three arches connected together, the middle one of which was higher and broader than the others: and all these three occupied a space only equal to the span of the lowest arch. Blank arcades were also much used in the exterior walls, as well as in the interior of rich Norman buildings; and some of the arches which composed them were often pierced for windows.

Q. What were the mouldings principally used in the decoration of Norman churches?

A. The chevron, or zig-zag, which is not always single, but often duplicated, triplicated, or quadrupled.

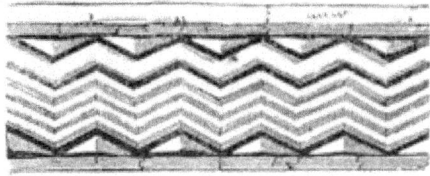

The reversed zig-zag.

The indented moulding.

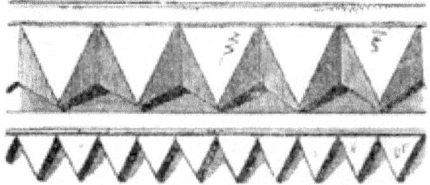

The embattled moulding.

The dovetail moulding.

The beak head.

The nebule, chiefly used for the fascia under a parapet.

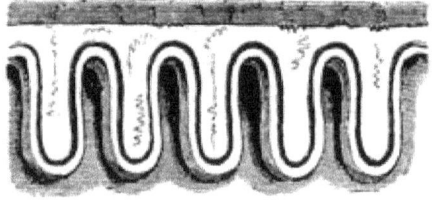

The billet.

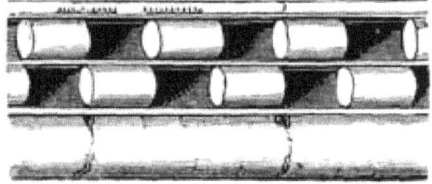

The square billet, or corbel bole, used for supporting a blocking course.

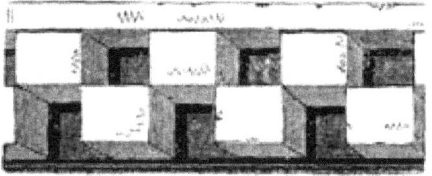

The cable moulding.

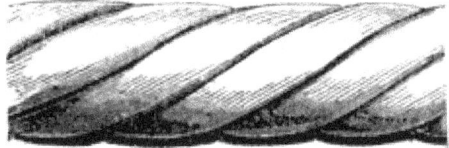

The double cone.

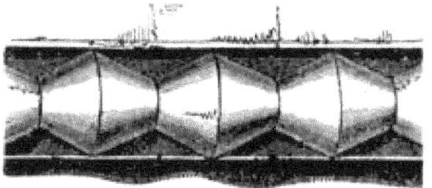

The pellet, or stud.

The hatched, or saw tooth.

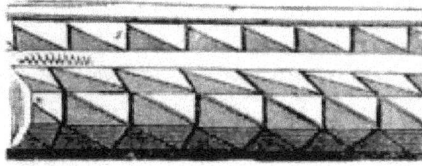

The nail head.

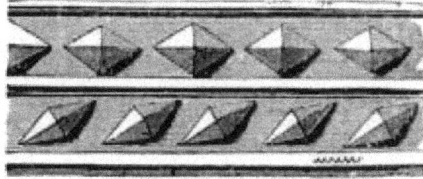

The lozenge.

The studded trellis.

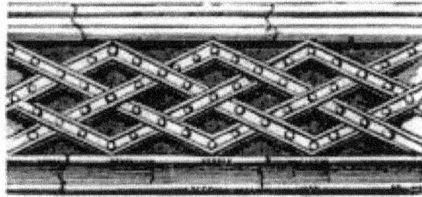

The diamond fret.

The medallion.

The star.

The scalloped or invected moulding.

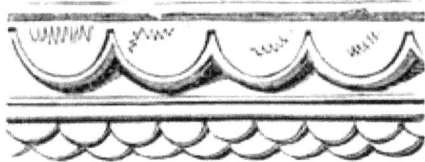

A variety of other mouldings and ornamental accessories are also to be met with, but those above described are the most common.

Q. What kind of string-course do we usually find carried along the walls of Norman churches, just below the windows?

A. A string-course similar in form to the common Norman abacus, with a plain face and the under part bevelled, is of most frequent occurrence; a plain semihexagon string-course is also often to be met with. Sometimes the string-course is ornamented with the zig-zag moulding.

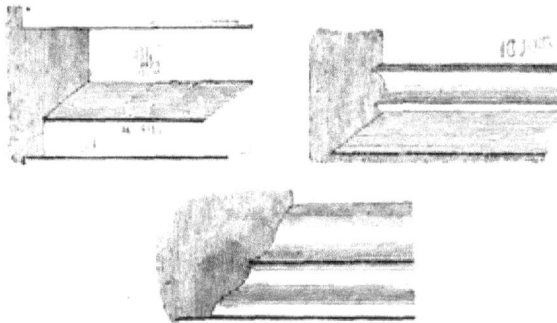

Norman Mouldings, from Binham Church, Norfolk, and Peterborough.

Q. What difference is there as to their general character and appearance between the early and late examples of Norman architecture?

A. The details of those buildings early in the style are characterized by their massiveness, simplicity, and plain appearance; the single or double-faced semicircular arches, both of doorways and windows, as well as the arches supporting the clerestory walls, are generally devoid of ornament, and the edges of the jambs and arches are square. The undercroft of Canterbury Cathedral, the work of Archbishop Lanfranc, between A. D.

1073 and A. D. 1080; the crypt and transepts of Winchester Cathedral, built by Bishop Walkelyn between A. D. 1079 and A. D. 1093; the plain Norman work of the Abbey Church at St. Alban's, built by Abbot Paul, between 1077-1093; and the north and south aisles of the choir of Norwich Cathedral, the work of Bishop Herbert, between A. D. 1096 and A. D. 1101, not to multiply examples, may be enumerated as instances of plain and early Norman work. In buildings late in the style we find a profusion of ornamental detail of a peculiar character, and numerous semi and tripartite cylindrical mouldings on the faces and edges of arches and vaulting-ribs. The transepts of Peterborough Cathedral, built by Abbot Waterville between A. D. 1155 and A. D. 1175, exhibit vaulting-groins faced with roll mouldings, and other details of an advanced stage; whilst the Galilee, Durham Cathedral, built by Bishop Pudsey, A. D. 1180, is remarkable for the lightness and elongation of the piers, which are formed of clustered columns; and the semicircular arches which spring from these are enriched both on the face and soffits with the chevron or zig-zag moulding. There are many intermediate gradations between the extreme plain and massive work of early date, and the enrichments, mouldings, and elongated proportions to be found late in the style; and in detail we may perceive an almost imperceptible merging into that style which succeeded the Norman.

Base. Crypt, St. Peter's, Oxford, c. 1100.

52-* Defunctus autem Rex beatissimus in crastino sepultus est Londini, in Ecclesia, quam ipse novo compositionis genere construxerat, a qua post, multi Ecclesias construentes, exemplum adepti, opus illud expensis œmulabantur sumptuosis.—MATT. PARIS.

Vesica Piscis in the tympan of the south doorway, Ely Cathedral

CHAPTER V.

OF THE SEMI-NORMAN STYLE.

Q. WHAT is the Semi-Norman style?

A. It is that style of transition which, without superseding the Norman style, prevailed more or less, in conjunction with it, during the latter part of the twelfth century, and probably even from an earlier period, and gradually led to the complete adoption, in the succeeding century, of the early pointed style in a pure state, and to the general disuse of the semicircular arch.

Q. By what is this style chiefly denoted?

A. By the intersection of semicircular arches, the frequent intermixture of the pointed arch in its incipient state with the semicircular arch, and the pointed arch with its accompaniments of features, mouldings, and ornamental accessories, exactly similar to those of the Norman style, both in its earlier and later gradations, and from which it appears to have differed only in the contour or form of the arch.

Early specimen of intersecting Arches, St. Botolph's Priory, Colchester.
(12th cent.)

Q. Whence are we to derive the origin of the pointed arch?

A. Many conjectural opinions on this much-contested question have been entertained, yet it still remains to be satisfactorily elucidated. Some would derive it from the East and ascribe its introduction to the Crusaders; some maintain that it was suggested by the intersection of semicircular arches, which intersection we frequently find in ornamental arcades; others contend that it originated from the mode of quadripartite vaulting adopted by the Normans, the segmental groins of which, crossing diagonally, produce to appearance the pointed arch; whilst some imagine it may have been derived from that mystical figure of a pointed oval form, the *Vesica Piscis*76-*. But whatever its origin, it appears to have been imperceptibly brought into partial use towards the middle of the twelfth century.

Semi-Norman double Piscina, Jesus College Chapel, Cambridge.

Q. What are the characteristics of this style?

A. In large buildings massive cylindrical piers support pointed arches, above which we often find round-headed clerestory windows, as at Buildwas Abbey Church, Salop; or semicircular arches forming the triforium, as at Malmesbury Abbey Church, Wilts. Sometimes we meet with successive tiers of arcades, in which the pointed arch is surmounted both by intersecting and semicircular arches, as in a portion of the west front of Croyland Abbey Church, Lincolnshire, now in ruins. The ornamental details and mouldings of this style generally partake of late Norman character; and the zig-zag and semicylindrical mouldings on the faces of arches appear to predominate, though other Norman mouldings are common; but we also frequently meet with specimens in the Semi-Norman style in which extreme plainness prevails, and the character is of that nature as to induce us to ascribe such buildings to rather an early period. Single and double, and sometimes even triple-faced arches, with the edges left square, distinguish plain specimens of this style from the plain-pointed double-faced arches of the succeeding century, the edges of which are splayed or chamfered. In late instances of this, as of the cotemporaneous Norman style, we observe in the details a gradual tendency to merge into those of the style of the thirteenth century, when the pointed arch had attained maturity, and the peculiar features and decorative mouldings and sculptures of Norman character had fallen into isuse.

Q. What specimen of this style is there of apparently early date?

Semi-Norman Arch, Abbey Church, Malmesbury.

A. The church, now in ruins, of Buildwas Abbey, Salop, founded A. D. 113579-*, is an early specimen of the Semi-Norman style, in which, with the incipient pointed arch, Norman features and details are blended. The nave is divided from the aisles by plain double-faced pointed arches, with square edges, and hood mouldings over, which spring from massive cylindrical piers with square bases and capitals; whilst the clerestory windows above (for there is no triforium) are semicircular-headed. The general features of early Norman character, the absence of decorative mouldings, and the plain appearance this church exhibits throughout, are such as perhaps to warrant the presumption that this church is the same structure mentioned in the charter of confirmation granted to this abbey by Stephen, A. D. 1138-9.

Q. What other noted specimens are there of this style?

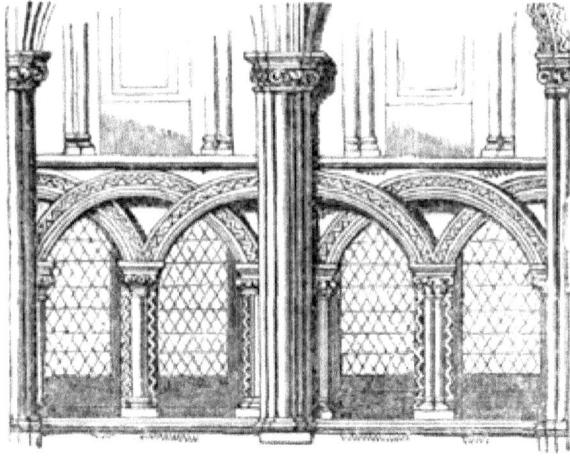

Intersecting Window Arches, St. Cross Church, Winchester.

A. The church of the Hospital of St. Cross, near Winchester, presents an interesting combination of semicircular, intersecting, and pointed arches, of cotemporaneous date, enriched with the zig-zag and other Norman decorative mouldings, and is a structure, in appearance and detail, of much later date than the church at Buildwas Abbey, though the same early era has been assigned to each.

St. Joseph's Chapel, Glastonbury, now in ruins, supposed to have been erected in the reigns of Henry the Second and Richard the First, is perhaps the richest specimen now remaining of the Semi-Norman or transition style, and is remarkable for the profusion of sculptured detail and combination of round and intersecting arches. In the remains of Malmesbury Abbey Church a Norman triforium with semicircular arches is supported on pointed arches which are enriched with Norman mouldings, and spring from massive cylindrical Norman piers. The interior of Rothwell Church, Northamptonshire, has much of Semi-Norman character: the aisles are divided from the nave by four lofty, plain, and triple-faced pointed arches, with square edges, springing from square piers with attached semicylindrical shafts on each side, and banded round midway between the bases and capitals; and the latter, which are enriched with sculptured foliage, are surmounted by square abaci; the west doorway is also of Semi-Norman character, and pointed, and is set within a projecting mass of masonry resembling the shallow Norman buttress. The circular part of St. Sepulchre's Church, Northampton, has early pointed arches, plain in design, springing from Norman cylindrical piers. In the circular part of the Temple Church, London, dedicated A. D. 1185, the piers consist of four clustered columns banded round midway between the bases and capitals, and approximating the Early English style of the thirteenth century; and these support pointed arches, over which and continued round the clerestory wall is an arcade of intersecting semicircular arches, and above these are round-headed windows.

Semi-Norman Window, Oxford Cathedral.

Q. What particular specimen of the Semi-Norman style has been noticed by any cotemporaneous author, and the date of it clearly defined?

A. The eastern part of Canterbury Cathedral, consisting of Trinity Chapel and the circular adjunct called Becket's Crown. The building of these commenced the year following the fire which occurred A. D. 1174, and was carried on without intermission for several successive years. Gervase, a monk of the cathedral, and an eyewitness of this re-edification, wrote a long and detailed description of the work in progress, and a comparison between that and the more ancient structure which was burnt; he does not, however, notice in any clear and precise terms the general adoption of the pointed arch and partial disuse of the round arch in the new building, from which we may perhaps infer they were at that period indifferently used, or rather that the pointed arch was gradually gaining the ascendancy83-*.

Q. How long does the Semi or Mixed Norman style appear to have prevailed?

Semi-Norman Arch, St. Cross Church, Winchester.

A. Though we can neither trace satisfactorily the exact period of its introduction, or even that of its final extinction, (for it appears to have merged gradually into the pure and unmixed pointed style of the thirteenth century,) we have perhaps no remains of this kind to which we can attribute an earlier date than that included between the years 1130 and 1140, unless we except the intersecting arches at St. Botulph's, Priory Church, Colchester, which may be a few years earlier; and it appears to have prevailed, in conjunction or intermixed with the Norman style, from thence to the close of the twelfth century, and probably to a somewhat later period.

Arcade, Christ Church, Oxford.

76-* The figure of a fish, whence the form *vesica piscis* originated, was one of the most ancient of the Christian symbols, emblematically significant of the word Ἰχθύς, which contained the initial letters of the name and titles of our Saviour. The symbolic representation of a fish we find sculptured on some of the sarcophagi of the early Christians discovered in the catacombs at Rome; but the actual figure of a fish afterwards gave place to an oval-shaped compartment, pointed at both extremities, bearing the same mystical signification as the fish itself, and formed by two circles intersecting each other in the centre. This was the most common symbol used in the middle ages, and thus delineated it abounds in Anglo-Saxon illuminated manuscripts. Every where we meet with it during the middle ages, in religious sculptures, in painted glass, on encaustic tiles, and on seals; and in the latter, that is, in those of many of the ecclesiastical courts, the form is yet retained. Even with respect to the origin of the pointed arch, that *vexata quæstio* of antiquaries, with what degree of probability may it not be attributed to this mystical form? It is indeed in this symbolical figure that we see the outline of the pointed arch plainly developed at least a century and half before the appearance of it in architectonic form. And in that age full of mystical significations, the twelfth century, when every part of a church was symbolized, it appears nothing strange if this typical form should have had its weight towards originating and determining the adoption of the pointed arch.—Internal Decorations of English Churches, British Critic, April, 1839.

79-* The date of the *foundation* of an abbey or church must not, however, be confounded with that of its actual *erection*, which was often many years later, and the only certain guide to which is the date of the *Consecration*.

83-* In the minute and circumstantial account which Gervase gives of the partial destruction of this cathedral by fire, A. D. 1174, and its after restoration, he seems to allude, though in obscure language, to the altered form of the vaulting in the aisles of the choir (*in circuitu extra chorum*); and his comparison, with reference to this building, between early and late Norman architecture is altogether so curious and exact as to deserve being transcribed:—

"Dictum est in superioribus quod post combustionem illam vetera fere omnia chori diruta sunt, et in quandam augustioris formæ transierunt novitatem. Nunc autem quæ sit operis utriusque differentia dicendum est. Pilariorum igitur tam veterum quam novorum una forma est, una et grossitudo, sed longitudo dissimilis. Elongati sunt enim pilarii novi longitudine pedum fere duodecim. In capitellis veteribus opus erat planum, in novis sculptura subtilis. Ibi in chori ambitu pilarii viginti duo, hic autem viginti octo. Ibi arcus et cætera omnia plana utpote sculpta secure et non scisello, his in omnibus fere sculptura idonea. Ibi columpna nulla marmorea, hic innumeræ. Ibi in circuitu extra chorum fornices planæ, hic arcuatæ sunt et clavatæ. Ibi murus super pilarios directus cruces a choro sequestrabat, hic vero nullo intersticio cruces a choro divisæ in unam clavem quæ in medio fornicis magnæ consistit, quæ quatuor pilariis principalibus innititur, convenire videntur. Ibi cœlum ligneum egregia pictura decoratum, hic fornix ex lapide et tofo levi decenter composita est. Ibi triforium unum, hic duo in choro, et in ala ecclesiæ tercium."—De Combust. et Repar. Cant. Ecclesiæ.

Doorway, Paulscray Church, Kent.

CHAPTER VI.

OF THE EARLY ENGLISH STYLE.

Q. DURING what era did the Early English style prevail?

A. It may be said to have prevailed generally throughout the thirteenth century86-*.

Q. How is it distinguished from the Norman and Semi-Norman styles?

A. The semicircular-headed arch, with its peculiar mouldings, was almost entirely discarded, and superseded by the pointed arch, with plain chamfered edges or mouldings of a different character. The segmental arch, nearly flat, was still however used in doorways, and occasionally the semicircular also, as in the arches of the Retrochoir, Chichester Cathedral.

Q. Of what three kinds were the pointed arches of this era?

A. The lancet, the equilateral, and the obtuse-angled arch.

Q. Which of these arches were most in use?

A. In large buildings the lancet and the equilateral-shaped arch were prevalent, as appears in Westminster Abbey, where the lancet arch predominates, and Salisbury Cathedral, where the equilateral arch is principally used; but in small country churches the obtuse-angled arch is most frequently found. All these arches are struck from two centres, and are formed from segments of a circle. In large buildings the architrave is faced with a succession of roll mouldings and deep hollows, in which the tooth ornament is sometimes inserted. In small churches the arches, which are double-faced, have merely plain chamfered edges.

Q. What was the difference of the piers between this and an earlier era?

A. Instead of the massive Norman, the Early English piers were, in large buildings, composed of an insulated column surrounded by slender detached shafts, all uniting together under one capital; these shafts were divided into parts by horizontal bands or fillets; but in small churches a plain octagonal pier, which can, however, scarcely be distinguished from that of a later style, predominated.

Q. How are the capitals distinguished?

A. They are simple in comparison with those of a later style, and are often bell-shaped, with a bead moulding round the neck, and a capping, with a series of mouldings, above; a very elegant and beautiful capital is frequently formed of stiffly sculptured foliage. The capital surmounting the multangular-shaped pier is also multangular in form, but plain, with a neck, and cap mouldings, and is difficult to be discerned from that of the succeeding style; the cap mouldings are, however, in general not so numerous as those of a later period.

Capital, Chapter House, Southwell.

Q. How are the doorways of this style distinguished?

A. The small doorways have generally a single detached shaft on each side, with a plain moulded bell-shaped capital, which is sometimes covered with foliage; and the architrave mouldings consist of a few simple members, with a hood moulding or label over, terminated by heads. We also find richer doorways with two or more detached shafts at the sides, and architrave mouldings composed of numerous members. Large doorways of the Early English style were sometimes double, being divided into two arched openings by a shaft, either single or clustered; and above this a quatrefoil was generally inserted, but sometimes the head was filled with sculptured detail. Examples of the double doorway occur in the cathedrals of Ely, Chichester, Wells, Salisbury, Lincoln, and Lichfield; also at Christchurch and St. Cross, Hants; Higham Ferrers, Northamptonshire; and in other large churches in this style.

Doorway, Baginton Church,
Warwickshire. (13th cent.)

Q. What kind of windows were prevalent?

Window, Beverley Minster. (13th cent.)

St. Giles's Oxford.   Ely cathedral.

A. In the early stages of this style the lancet arch-headed window, very long and narrow, was prevalent; frequently two, three, or more of these were connected together by hood mouldings, the middle window rising higher than those at the sides; sometimes they were unconnected, and without hood mouldings. In the east wall of Early English chancels three lancet windows, thus arranged, are frequently displayed. At a later period a broader window, divided into two lights by a plain mullion, finished at the top with a lozenge or circle, was used; and sometimes a window divided into three lights, the middle one higher than the others, and comprised under one hood moulding, was in use; windows of four and even five lancet lights, thus disposed, are to be met with, but are not common; the sides of the windows were in general simply splayed, without mouldings, and increased in width inwardly, but slender shafts were sometimes annexed; and we also find, in the interior of rich buildings of this style, detached shafts standing out in front of the stonework forming the window jambs, and supporting the arch of the window. Towards the close of this style the windows assumed a more ornamental cast, and became much larger, being frequently divided into two or four principal lights, with one or three circles in the heads; both the lights and circles are foliated, and these evince the transition in progress to the next, or Decorated style. Beneath the windows a string-course is generally carried horizontally along the wall; and a roll moulding, similar to the upper members of the string-course of Merton College Chapel, Oxford, is most commonly met with, as the string-course.

Interior of Window, St. Giles's, Oxford.

Q. How is the buttress of this age distinguished?

A. In general by its plain triangular or pedimental head, its projecting more from the building than the Norman buttress, and from its being less in breadth. It is also sometimes carried up above the parapet wall. The edges of the buttresses are sometimes chamfered; and plain buttresses in stages finished with simple slopes are not uncommon. We very rarely find buttresses of this style disposed at the angles of buildings, though such disposition was common in the succeeding style; but two buttresses placed at right angles with each other, and with the face of the wall, generally occur at the angles of churches in this style. Flying buttresses were sometimes used to strengthen the clerestory walls of large buildings, and have a light and elegant effect.

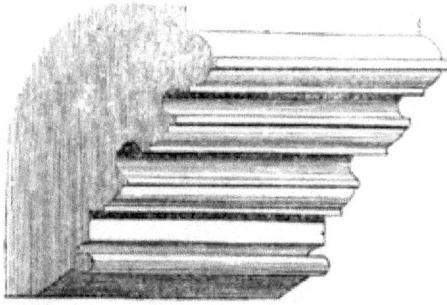

String-Course, Merton College Chapel, Oxford.

Q. Were the walls differently built?

A. They were not so thick as those of an earlier period, which occasioned the want of stronger buttresses to support them.

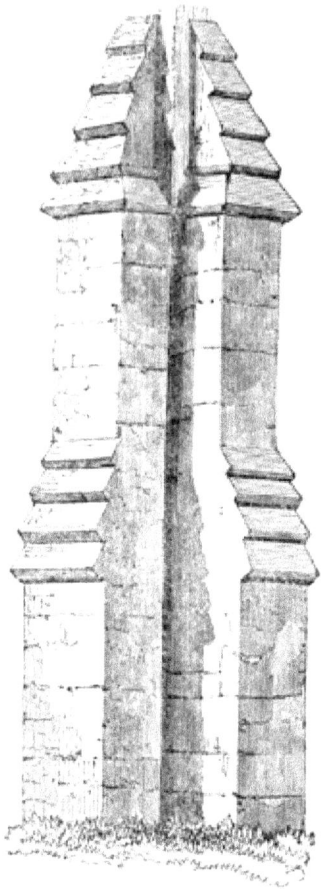

Pottern, Wilts.   Hartlepool, Durham.

     Q. Were the Early English roofs of a different construction from those of a later style?

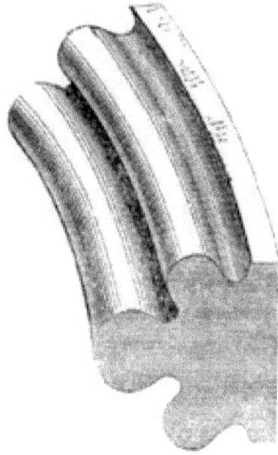

Groining Rib, Salisbury Cathedral.

A. The Norman and Early English roofs were high and acutely pointed. The original roofs of most of our old churches, from their exposure to the weather, have long since fallen to decay, and been replaced by others of a more obtuse shape; but in general the height and angular form of the original roof may be ascertained by the weather moulding still remaining on the side of the tower or steeple. The interior vaulting of stone roofs was composed of fewer parts and ribs, which were often not more numerous than those of Norman vaulting, and does not present that complexity of arrangement which occurs in the vaulting-ribs of subsequent styles. In the cathedral of Salisbury also in the nave of Wells Cathedral are simple and good examples of Early English vaulting. A curious groined roof, in which the ribs are of wood—plain, cut with chamfered edges—and the cells of the vaulting are covered with boards, is to be met with in the church of Warmington, Northamptonshire, a very rich, perfect, and interesting specimen of this style.

Q. Was not the spire introduced at this period?

A. Yes, many spires were then built; among which was that of old St. Paul's Cathedral, more than five hundred feet high, and which was destroyed by fire, A. D. 1561. The spire of Oxford Cathedral is also of this style. Early English spires are generally what are called Broach spires, and spring at once from the external face of the walls of the tower, without any intervening parapet.

Q. Whence did the spire take its origin?

A. It appears to have been suggested by the Norman pinnacle, which, at first a conical capping, afterwards became polygonal, and ribbed at the angles, thus presenting the prototype of the spire.

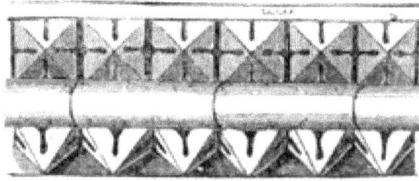

Q. What ornament is peculiar, or nearly so, to this style?

A. That called the tooth or dog-tooth ornament, a kind of pyramidal-shaped flower of four leaves, which is generally inserted in a hollow moulding, and, when seen in profile, presents a zig-zag or serrated appearance. The tooth moulding appears to have been introduced towards the close of the twelfth century; and an early instance where it occurs is on a late Norman doorway, at Whitwell Church, Rutlandshire: we do not, however, meet with it in buildings of a later style than that of the thirteenth century. It is sometimes found used in great profusion in doorways, windows, and other ornamental details; but many churches of this style are entirely devoid of this ornament. The ball-flower, though introduced in the thirteenth century, is not a common ornament until the fourteenth, to which era it may be said more particularly to belong; we find it in cornice mouldings, and sometimes on capitals.

Q. What may be observed of the sculptured foliage of this style?

A. As applied to capitals, bases, crockets, and other ornamental detail, we find the general design and appearance of the sculptured foliage of this style to be stiff and formal compared with that of the succeeding style, when the arrangement of the foliage more closely approximated nature, and a greater freedom both in conception and execution was evinced.

Boss of Sculptured Foliage, Warmington Church, Northamptonshire.

Q. How are the parapets distinguished?

A. They are often plain and embattled; but sometimes a simple horizontal parapet is used, supported by a corbel table, as in the tower of Haddenham Church, Buckinghamshire, and on that of Brize Norton Church, Oxfordshire. At Salisbury Cathedral the parapet is relieved by a series of blank trefoil headed pannels, sunk in the face.

Q. What may be said in general terms of the style of the thirteenth century, in comparing it with the styles which immediately preceded and followed it?

Parapet, Salisbury Cathedral.

A. In comparison with the Norman style, with its heavy concomitants and enrichments, the style of the thirteenth century is light and simple, and the details possess much elegance of contour. These, in small buildings, are generally plain; but in large buildings they exhibit numerous mouldings, combined with a certain degree of decorative embellishment. This style is, however, far from presenting that extreme beauty of outline and tasteful conception, combined with the pure and chaste ornamental accessories, which prevail in the designs of the fourteenth century.

Q. What particular structures may be noticed as belonging to this style?

A. Salisbury Cathedral, built by Bishop Poore between A. D. 1220 and 1260, is perhaps the most perfect specimen, on a large scale, of this style in its early state, with narrow lancet windows; the nave and transepts of Westminster Abbey, commenced in 1245, exhibit this style in a more advanced stage; whilst Lincoln Cathedral is, for the most part, a rich specimen of this style in its late or transition state. The west front of Wells Cathedral, erected by the munificence of Bishop Joceline, between A. D. 1213 and A. D. 1239, is covered with blank arcades and a number of trefoil-headed niches, surmounted by plain pedimental canopies, which contain specimens of statuary remarkable for their extreme beauty and freedom of design.

Corbel, Wells Cathedral.

86-* From the economic principles on which our modern churches are, with few exceptions, planned, they are mostly designed after and are intended to resemble in style those of the thirteenth century, in which more detail can be dispensed with than in any other style. Hence it follows that the just proportions and adaptation of the different parts and the minutest details and mouldings in ancient churches of this style required to be carefully studied, more so perhaps for practical purposes than in churches of any other style.

Dunchurch Church, Warwickshire.

CHAPTER VII.

OF THE DECORATED ENGLISH STYLE.

Q. WHEN did the Decorated English style commence, and how long did it prevail?

A. It may be said to have commenced in the latter part of the thirteenth century, or reign of Edward the First, and to have prevailed about a century. The transition from the Early English style to this, and again from this to the succeeding style, was however so extremely gradual, that it is difficult to affix any precise date for the termination of one style, or the introduction of another.

Bracket, York Cathedral.

Q. Whence does it derive its appellation?

A. From there being a greater redundancy of chaste ornament in this than in the preceding style; and though it does not exhibit that extreme multiplicity of decorative detail as the style of the fifteenth century, the general contours and forms which this style presents, and the principal lines of composition, which verge pyramidically rather than vertically or horizontally, are infinitely more pleasing; and it is justly considered as the most beautiful style of English ecclesiastical architecture.

Q. What difference is there between the arches of this style, which support the clerestory, and those of an earlier period?

A. The lancet arch is seldom seen; the equilateral arch is generally, though not always, used. Both this and the obtuse-angled arch are, taken exclusively, difficult to be distinguished from those of an earlier period. In small buildings the edges of the pier arches are plain and chamfered. In large churches a series of quarter-round or roll-mouldings, which have often a square-edged fillet attached, are applied to the sub-arch, edges, and facing.

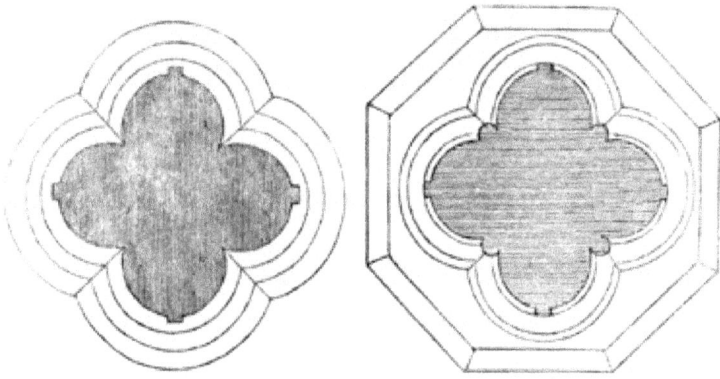

Section of Piers rom Grendon Church, Warwickshire, and Austrey Church, Warwickshire.

Q. What difference occurs in the piers from which these arches spring?

A. In large buildings piers of this style were composed of a cluster of slender cylindrical shafts, not standing detached from each other, as in the Early English style, but closely united. A common pier of this kind is formed of four shafts thus united, without bands, with a square-edged fillet running vertically up the face of each shaft. Sometimes a simple cylindrical pier is found. The octagonal pier, with plain sides, is very prevalent in small churches, and does not differ materially from the Early English pier of the same kind. The capitals are either bell-shaped, clustered, or octagonal, to correspond with the shape of the piers; but the cap mouldings are more numerous than in the earlier style. Sometimes the capitals are sculptured. In the churches of Monkskirby, Warwickshire, and of Cropredy, Oxfordshire, the arches which support the clerestory spring at once from the piers, without any intervening capitals, a practice not uncommon in the style of the fifteenth century, but very rare in this.

Q. How are the vaulted roofs of this style distinguished?

A. Of the large stone vaulted roofs each bay is intersected by longitudinal, transverse, and diagonal ribs, with shorter ribs springing from the bearing shafts intervening; thus forming a series of vaulting cells more numerous than are to be met with in the Early English style, though not subdivided to the excess observable in the vaulted roofs of the fifteenth century. Sculptured bosses often occur at the intersections. In the nave of York Cathedral, finished about A. D. 1330, the groining of the roof is less complicated than that of the choir of the same cathedral, constructed between A. D. 1360 and A. D. 1370106-*. Small structures are more simply vaulted. In a chantry chapel adjoining the north side of the chancel of Willingham Church, Cambridgeshire, is a very acute-pointed angular-shaped stone roof, the plain surface of the vaulting of which is supported by two pointed arches springing from corbels projecting from the walls; and these sustain straight-sided stone vaulting ribs, obliquely disposed to conform with the angle of the roof, and which act as principals; and above each arch, and between that and the ridge-line of the oblique ribs or principals, the space is filled with an open quatrefoil and other tracery. The north transept of Limington Church, Somersetshire, has a high pitched stone roof supported by groined ribs.

Q. Are there many wooden roofs of this style remaining?

A. We find comparatively few original wooden roofs in structures of the fourteenth century, for such have generally been superseded by roofs of a later date and of a more obtuse form. The high and acute pitch of the original roof is, however, still generally discernible by the weather moulding on the east wall of the tower. In the nave of Higham Ferrars Church, Northamptonshire, is a wooden roof which apparently belongs to this style: the roof is angular-pointed and open to the ridge-line, the walls are connected by tie-beams, and under each of these is a wooden arch formed of two ribs or beams springing from stone corbels.

Q. In what respect do the doors of this style differ?

Window, Dunchurch Church, Warwickshire.

A. Large doorways of this style have lateral shafts, with capitals, and between the shafts architrave mouldings intervene, which run without stop into the base tablet: of such the south doorway of St. Martin's Church, Leicester, is an instance. Small doorways are generally without shafts, but have a series of quarter-round, semicylindrical, and tripartite roll mouldings at the sides, which are continuous with the architrave mouldings; and these have sometimes a square-edged fillet on the face. The doorways of this style are frequently enriched with pedimental and ogee-shaped canopies, ornamented with crockets and finials; of which the north doorway of Exeter Cathedral and the south doorway of Everdon Church, Northamptonshire, may be cited as examples. Large doorways have sometimes a double opening, divided by a clustered shaft, as in the entrance to the Chapter House, York Cathedral. In some instances the head of the doorway is foliated, and we observe in detail an approximation to the succeeding style. The west doorway of Dunchurch Church, Warwickshire, is in this stage of transition.

Q. How are the windows of this style known?

Square-headed Decorated Window, Ashby Folville, Leicestershire.

A. In the later stage of the Early English style the windows became enlarged, and the heads were filled with foliated circles. To these succeeded, in the fourteenth century, windows ornamented with geometrical and flowing tracery, peculiarities which exclusively pertain to this style, and by which it is most easily known. The windows are of good proportions, and are divided into two or more principal lights by mullions, which at the spring of the arch form designs of regular geometrical construction, or branch out into flowing ramifications composing flame-like compartments, which are foliated109-*. The variety of tracery in windows of this style is very great, and they frequently have pedimental and ogee canopies over them, ornamented in the same manner as those over doors: examples of this kind may be found at York Cathedral. In the south transept of Chichester, and west front of Exeter Cathedrals, are two exceeding large and beautiful windows of this style; the first filled with geometrical, the other with flowing, tracery. In some windows of this style the mullions simply cross in the head, as in a later style, but the lights are commonly foliated, and the difference may in general be discerned by the mouldings: such windows occur in Stoneleigh Church, Warwickshire. There are also many square-headed windows in this style, distinguished by the flowing tracery in the heads, and by other characteristic marks: of such a window in Ashby Folville Church, Leicestershire, is a rich and good example. Circular windows, filled with tracery, are not uncommon in large buildings; and we also meet with triangular spherical-shaped windows, as in the clerestory of Barton Segrave Church, Northamptonshire111-*.

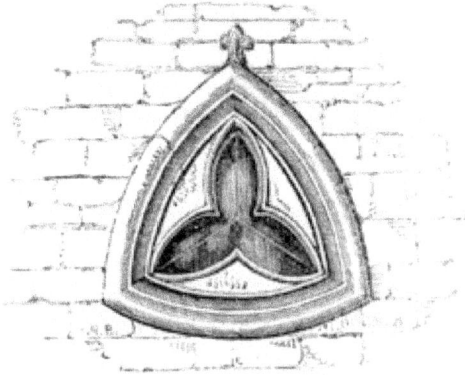

Window, Barton Segrave Church.

Q. Of what description are the mouldings which pertain to this style?

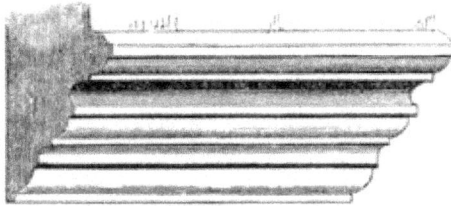

Moulding, Dunchurch Church, Warwickshire.

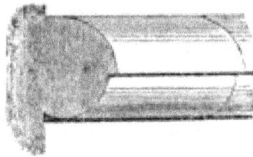

Roll Moulding, Chacombe Church, Northamptonshire.

String-Course, Sedgeberrow Church, Gloucestershire.

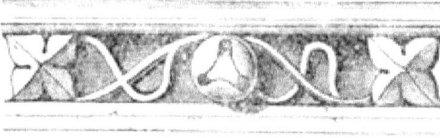

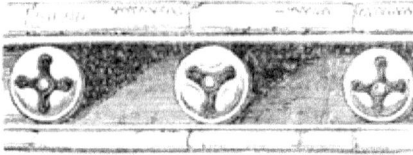

Ball-Flower Ornament,
Bloxham Church, Oxfordshire, and York Cathedral.

A. They approximate more nearly, in section and appearance, those of the thirteenth than those of the fifteenth century, but the members are generally more numerous than in those of the former style; quarter-round, half, and tripartite cylinder mouldings, often filleted along the face and divided by small cavetto mouldings, sometimes deeply cut, are common. The string-course under the windows frequently consists, as in the preceding style, of a simple roll moulding, the upper member of which overlaps the lower. A plain semicylindrical moulding, with a square-edged fillet on the face, is also common, and occurs at the church of Orton-on-the-Hill, Leicestershire. The hood moulding over the windows often consists of a quarter-round or ogee, with a cavetto beneath, and sometimes returns horizontally along the walls as a string-course; a disposition, however, more frequently observable in the Early English style than in this: of such disposition the churches of Harvington, Worcestershire, and of Sedgeberrow, Gloucestershire, may be cited as affording examples. In decorative work we often meet with the ball-flower, one of the most characteristic ornaments of the style, consisting of a ball inclosed within three or four leaves, and sometimes bearing a resemblance to the rose-bud, inserted at intervals in a cavetto or hollow moulding, with the accompaniment, in some instances, of foliage; a four-leaved flower, inserted in the same manner, is also not uncommon.

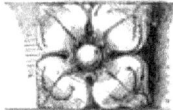

Decorated Buttress, St. Mary Magdalen, Oxford.

Q. How may the buttresses of this style be distinguished?

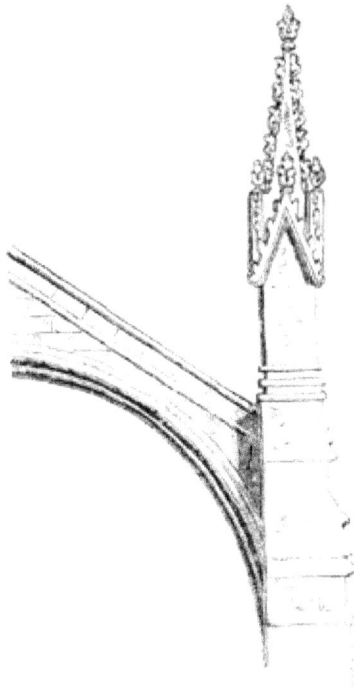

Flying Buttress, Salisbury Cathedral.

A. They were worked in stages, and their set-offs have frequently triangular heads, sometimes plain but often ornamented with crockets and finials of a more decorative character than those of the Early English style. Many buttresses have, however, plain slopes as set-offs, and they are frequently placed diagonally at the corners of buildings, as at Dunchurch Church, Warwickshire. The flying buttresses at Salisbury Cathedral, in which the thrust is partly counterpoised by pyramidal-headed pinnacles decorated with crockets and finials, are of this age.

Q. What parapet is peculiar to this style?

A. Besides the plain embattled parapet, which is not always easy to be distinguished from other styles, a horizontal blocking course, pierced with foliated or wavy, flowing tracery, which has a rich effect, is common. Of this description specimens occur at St. Mary Magdalen Church, Oxford, and Brailes Church, Warwickshire.

Q. What is observable in the niches of this style?

A. They are very beautiful, and are generally surmounted by triangular or ogee-shaped canopies, enriched with crockets and finials, while the interior of the canopies are groined with numerous small rib mouldings.

The crockets and finials of this style, as decorative embellishments, are peculiarly graceful, chaste, and pleasing in contour.

Q. Was the transition from this style to the next gradual?

A. Both the transition from the Early English to the Decorated style, and from the Decorated to the Florid or Perpendicular, was so gradual, that though many individual details and ornaments were extremely dissimilar, and peculiar to each particular style, we are only able to judge from examples when a change was generally established.

Q. From what cotemporary writers of the fourteenth century can we collect any architectural notices, either general or of detail?

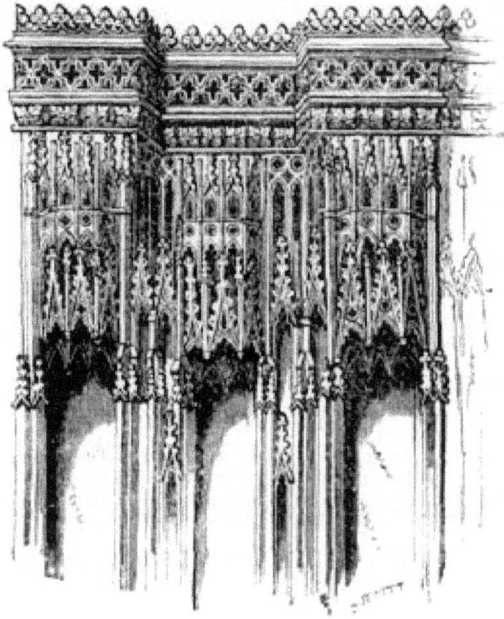

Part of the Altar Screen, Winchester Cathedral.

A. In Chaucer we find allusions made to *imageries, pinnacles, tabernacles,* (canopied niches for statuary,) and *corbelles*. Lydgate, in *The Siege of Troy*, in his description of the buildings, adverts to those of his own age, and uses several architectural terms now obsolete or little understood, and some which are not so, as *gargoiles*. In Pierce Ploughman's Creed we have a concise but faithful description of a large monastic edifice of the fourteenth century, comprising the church or minster, cloister, chapter house, and other offices.

Q. What edifices maybe noticed as constructed in this style?

A. In Exeter Cathedral this style may be said generally to prevail, although some portions are of earlier and some of later date. Great part of Lichfield Cathedral was also built during the fourteenth century. The beautiful cloisters adjoining Norwich Cathedral, commenced A. D. 1297, but not finished for upwards of a century, although proceeded with by different prelates from time to time, rank as the most beautiful of the kind we have remaining. Several country churches are wholly or principally erected in this style. Broughton Church, Oxfordshire, may be instanced as an elegant, pleasing, and complete example of plain decorated work. Trumpington Church, Cambridgeshire, is also deserving of notice; and Wimington Church, Bedfordshire, built by John Curteys, lord of the manor, who died A. D. 1391, is a small but late edifice in the Decorated style. Annexations were also made during this century to numerous churches of earlier construction, by the erection of additional aisles or chapels as chantries. In all these structures we find more or less, in general appearance, form, and detail, of that extreme beauty and elegance of design which prevailed, as it were, for about a century, and then imperceptibly glided away.

Parapet, Magdalen Church, Oxford.

106-* The allusion is made to the vaulted roofs of the nave and choir of this cathedral as they existed previous to the late unfortunate and destructive fires.

109-* The Flamboyant window, common in France, is not often met with in this country. On the north side of Salford Church, Warwickshire, is, however, a window of this description, filled with flamboyant tracery.

111-* For specimens of Decorated windows with flowing tracery in the heads, vide cuts, pp. 12 and 13.

South Porch of Newbold-upon-Avon Church, Warwickshire.

CHAPTER VIII.

OF THE FLORID OR PERPENDICULAR ENGLISH STYLE.

Q. WHEN may this style be said to have commenced, and how long did it prevail?

A. We find traces of it in buildings erected at the close of the reign of Edward the Third (circa A. D. 1375); and it prevailed for about a century and half, or rather more, till late in the reign of Henry the Eighth (circa A. D. 1539).

Q. Whence does it derive its appellation?

A. From the multiplicity, profusion, and minuteness of its ornamental detail, it has by some received the designation of FLORID; by others, from the mullions of the windows and the divisions of ornamental panel-work running in straight or perpendicular lines up to the head, which is not the case in any earlier style, it has been called and is now better known by the designation of the PERPENDICULAR121-*.

Q. In what respects did it differ from the style which immediately preceded it?

A. The beautiful flowing contour of the lines of tracery characteristic of the Decorated style was superseded by mullions and transoms, and, in panel-work, lines of division disposed vertically and horizontally; and in lieu of the quarter-round, semi and tripartite roll and small hollow mouldings of the fourteenth century, angular-edged mouldings with bold cavettos became predominant.

Q. Of what kind are the arches of this style?

A. Although, in this style, pointed arches constructed from almost every radius are to be found, the complex four-centred arch, commonly called the Tudor arch, was almost peculiar to it; and the cavetto or wide and rather shallow hollow moulding, a characteristic feature of this style, often appears in the architrave mouldings of pier arches, doorways, and windows, and as a cornice moulding under parapets.

Window, St. Mary's Church, Oxford.

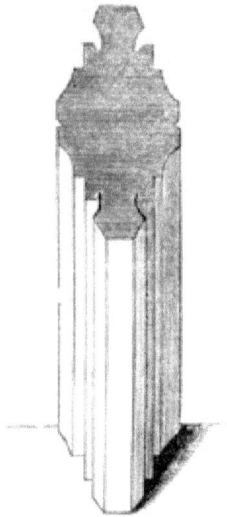

Mullion, Burford Church, Oxfordshire.

Q. How are the piers of this style, which support the clerestory arches, distinguished from those of an earlier period?

Capital, Piddleton Church, Dorsetshire.

A. The section of a pier, which is common in this style, may be described as formed from a square or parallelogram, with the angles fluted or cut in a bold hollow, and on the flat face of each side of the pier a semicylindrical shaft is attached. The flat faces or sides of the pier and the hollow mouldings at the angles are carried up vertically from the base moulding to the spring of the arch, and thence, without the interposition of any capital, in a continuous sweep to the apex of the arch; but the slender shafts attached to the piers have capitals, the upper members of which are angular-shaped. The base mouldings are also polygonal. Piers and arches of this description are numerous, and occur, amongst other churches, in St. Thomas Church, Salisbury; Cerne Abbas Church, Bradford Abbas Church, and Piddleton Church, Dorsetshire; Yeovil Church, Somersetshire; and Burford Church, Oxfordshire. In some churches a very slender shaft with a capital is attached to each angle of the pier, which is disposed lozengewise, the main body of the pier presenting continuous lines of moulding with those of the arch, unbroken by any capital: as in the piers of Bath Abbey Church, rebuilt early in the sixteenth century. In small country churches we frequently find the architrave mouldings of the arch continued down the piers, which are altogether devoid of any horizontal stop by way of capital. The churches of Brinklow and Willoughby, in Warwickshire, afford instances of this kind. Piers somewhat different to those above described are also to be met with, but are not so common.

Q. What else may be noted respecting some of the piers and arches in this style?

A. The face of the sub-arch or soffit is sometimes enriched with oblong panelled compartments, arched-headed and foliated; and these are continued down the inner sides of the piers. The arches of the tower of Cerne Abbas Church, Dorsetshire, and some of the arches in Sherborne Church, in the same county, may be instanced as examples.

Panelled Arch, Sherborne Church, Dorsetshire.

Q. How may we distinguish the doorways and doors of this style?

A. Many doorways of this style, especially during its early progress, were surmounted by crocketted ogee-shaped hood mouldings, terminating with finials. In the most common doorway of this style, however, the depressed four-centred arch appears within a square head, and in general a rectangular hood moulding over; and the spandrels or spaces between the spring and apex of the arch and angles of the square head over it are filled with quatrefoils, panelling, foliage, small shields, or other sculptured ornaments. Sometimes the depressed four-centred arch appears without any hood moulding, and we occasionally meet with a simple pointed arch described from two centres placed within a rectangular compartment. Doorways in this style are often profusely ornamented; and it is common to see doors covered with panel-work boldly recessed, the compartments of which are sometimes filled in the heads with crocketed ogee arches, which produce a rich effect.

Doorway, All Souls College, Oxford.

Q. Are there many fine porches of this style?

A. More than in any other style, and they are often profusely enriched, the front and sides being covered with panel-work, tracery, and niches for statuary. The interior of the roof is frequently groined, sometimes with fan tracery, but generally with simple though numerous ribs; and in many instances a room is constructed over the groined entrance or lower story of the porch, but so as to be in keeping with and form part of the general design. The south porch of Gloucester Cathedral, the south-west porch of Canterbury Cathedral, the south porch of St. John's Church, Cirencester, and the south porch of Burford Church, Oxfordshire, may be noticed as examples of rich porches of this style; many others might also be enumerated, as they are very numerous and various in detail. Some porches are comparatively plain, as the south porch of the church of Newbold-upon-Avon, Warwickshire.

Q. How are the windows distinguished?

Window, New College Chapel, Oxford.

A. The chief characteristic in the windows of this style, and which renders them easily distinguished from those of an earlier era, consists in the vertical bearing of the mullions, which, instead of diverging off in flowing lines, are carried straight up into the head of the window; smaller mullions spring from the heads of the principal lights, and thus the upper portion of the window is filled with panel-like compartments. The principal as well as the subordinate lights are foliated in the heads; and in large windows the lights are often divided horizontally by transoms, which are sometimes embattled. From the continued upright position of the mullions and tracery-bars is derived the term PERPENDICULAR, as applied to this style. The forms of the window-arches vary from the simple pointed to the complex four-centred arch, more or less depressed. The windows of the clerestory are sometimes arched, but oftener square-headed; and some large windows of the latter description nearly cover the sides of the clerestory walls of Chipping Norton Church, Oxfordshire.

Q. What do we frequently observe in buildings of this style?

A. The interior walls of churches are often completely covered with panel-work tracery, arched headed and foliated, from the clerestory windows down to the mouldings of the arches below. The walls of Sherborne Church, Dorsetshire, present in the interior a surface almost entirely covered with panel-work. Several large churches in this style have also long ranges of clerestory windows, set so close to each other that the whole length of the clerestory wall seems perforated: we may enumerate as examples the churches of St. Michael, Coventry; Stratford-upon-Avon, Warwickshire; and Lavenham and Melford, Suffolk. Walls covered on the exterior with panel-work are also far from uncommon: the Abbots' Tower, Evesham, the tower of the church of St. Neot's, Huntingdonshire, and of Wrexham, Denbighshire, and many other rich towers, (especially those of the churches in Somersetshire, where rich specimens in this style abound, more so perhaps than in any other county,) are thus decorated. The exterior of many rich structures in this style are also covered with panel-work, as the Beauchamp Chapel, Warwick, the west front of Winchester Cathedral, and Henry the Seventh's Chapel, Westminster Abbey.

Parapet, St. Peter's Church, Oxford.

Q. How are the vaulted roofs of this style distinguished?

A. They are in detail more complicated than those of earlier styles, and in plain as distinguished from fan-tracery vaulting the groining ribs are more numerous. The ribs often diverge at different angles, and form geometrical-shaped panels or compartments; and the design has, in some instances, been assimilated to net-work. Plain vaulting of this style occurs in the nave and choir, Norwich Cathedral; the Lady Chapel and choir, Gloucester Cathedral; the nave, Winchester Cathedral; the Beauchamp Chapel, Warwick; and a very late specimen in the choir, Oxford Cathedral. A very rich and peculiar description of vaulting is one composed of pendant semicones covered with foliated panel-work, and, from the design resembling a fan spread open, called *fan-tracery*. Of this description of vaulting an early instance appears in the cloisters, Gloucester Cathedral. The roofs of King's College Chapel, Cambridge, and Henry the Seventh's Chapel, Westminster Abbey, are well-known examples; and portions of several of our cathedrals and many small chantry and sepulchral chapels are thus vaulted.

Q. What may be observed of the wooden roofs of this style?

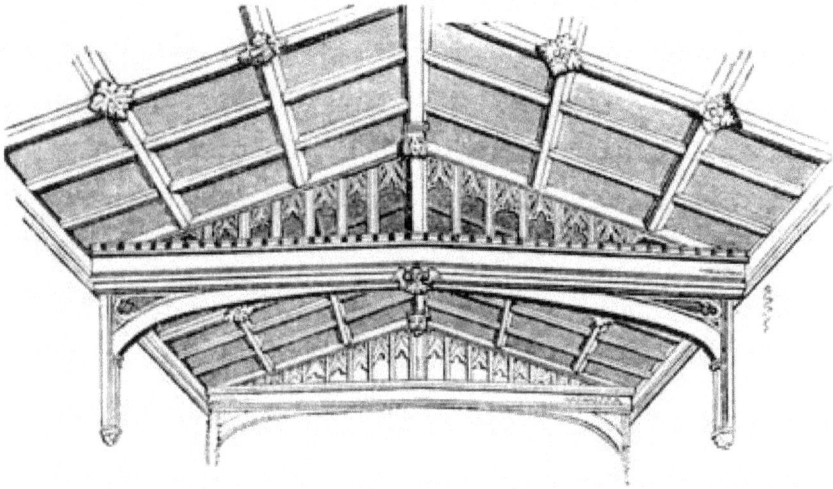

Wooden Roof, south aisle, St. Mary's Church, Leicester.

A. They are far more numerous than those we meet with in all the previous styles; and we frequently find churches of early date in which the original roofs, having perhaps become decayed, have been removed and replaced by roofs designed in that style prevalent during the fifteenth century. The slope or pitch of the roof is much lower than before, and the form altogether more obtuse, and sometimes approaching nearly to flatness. The exterior is on this account often entirely concealed from view by the parapet. Many roofs of this style are divided into bays or compartments by horizontal tie-beams faced with mouldings, and apparently supported by curved ribs springing from corbels, and forming spandrels filled with open worked tracery; and the spaces between the tie-beam, the king-post, and the sloping rafters of the roof, are filled with pierced or open-work tracery. The sloping bays or compartments of the roof are divided by rib mouldings into squares or parallelograms of panel-work, which are again often subdivided into similar-shaped panels by smaller ribs with carved bosses at the intersections. Some roofs are nearly flat, and simply panelled. On many roofs traces of painting and gilding may still be discerned, more especially in that part which was over an altar, and where the roof often bears indications of having been more ornamented than other parts. Roofs painted of an azure colour and studded with gilt stars are not uncommon. Sometimes the roof is coved, and the boards are painted in imitation of clouds. A great variety of wooden roofs is to be met with in this style, many of them exceeding rich; whilst the cornice under the roof is sometimes elaborately carved and enriched. Some roofs are much plainer in construction than others; and it was, during this era, a part of the church on the enrichment of which no small expense and attention were bestowed.

Q. What may be noted respecting the parapets of this era?

Parapet, St. Peter's Church, Dorchester.

A. Many embattled parapets are covered with sunk or pierced panelling, and ornamented with quatrefoils or small trefoil-headed arches; and they have sometimes triangular-shaped heads, as at King's College Chapel, Cambridge, and at the east end of Peterborough Cathedral. We also find horizontal or straight-sided parapets, covered with sunk or pierced quatrefoils in circles. A plain embattled parapet, with the horizontal coping moulding continued or carried down the sides of the embrasures, and then again returning horizontally, as at St. Peter's Church, Dorchester, Dorsetshire, is also common. A bold but shallow cavetto or hollow cornice moulding is frequently carried along the wall just under the parapet.

Q. Was the panelled or sunk quatrefoil much used in decorative detail?

A. In rich buildings of this style the base, the parapet, and other intermediate portions were decorated with rows or bands of sunk quatrefoils, sometimes inclosed in circles, sometimes in squares, and sometimes in lozenge-shaped compartments.

Rose and Foliage, Henry VII.'s Chapel, Westminster Abbey.

Q. What other ornamental detail is peculiar to this style?

A. The rose, which, differing only in colour, was the badge both of the houses of York and Lancaster, and as such is often to be met with. Rows of a trefoil or lozenge-shaped leaf, somewhat like an oak or strawberry leaf, with a smaller trefoil more simple in design intervening between two larger, was frequently used as a finish to the cornice of rich screen-work, and is known under the designation of *the Tudor Flower.* It is also common to find the tendrils, leaves, and fruit of the vine carved or sculptured in great profusion in the hollow of rich cornice mouldings, especially on screen-work in the interior of a church.

Vine Leaves and Fruit, Whitchurch Church, Somersetshire.

Q. In what respect do the mouldings of this style differ from those of earlier styles?

A. In a greater prevalence of angular forms, which may be observed in noticing the section of a series of mouldings, and in the bases and capitals of cylindrical shafts. A large and bold but shallow hollow moulding or cavetto, in which, when forming part of a horizontal fascia or cornice, flowers, leaves, and other sculptured details are often inserted at intervals, is a common feature; and such moulding, without any insertion, is frequent in doorway and window jambs. A kind of double ogee moulding with little projection, is, in conjunction with other mouldings, also of common occurrence.

Window, St. Peter's Church, Oxford.

Q. Of what particular description of work do we find the existing remains to be almost entirely designed and executed in this style of ecclesiastical art?

A. Of the numerous specimens of rich wooden screens, composed as to the lower part of sunk panelling, with open work above, which we often find separating the chancel from the body of the church, supporting the rood-loft, and inclosing chantry chapels in side aisles, comparatively few now remaining are of an earlier date than the fifteenth century137-*.

Q. What do we find in large buildings erected late in this style?

A. Octagonal turrets, plain or covered with sunk panelling, and surmounted with ogee-headed cupolas, which are adorned with crockets and finials. In Henry the Seventh's Chapel, Westminster, they are used as buttresses. We also find them at King's College Chapel, Cambridge; at St. George's Chapel, Windsor; and at Winchester Cathedral.

Q. Have we any coeval documents which contain particulars relating to the erection of churches?

A. The contract entered into A. D. 1412, for the building of Catterick Church, Yorkshire, and the contract entered into A. D. 1435, for rebuilding, as it now stands, the collegiate church of Fotheringhay in Northamptonshire, or copies of such, have been preserved; as have particulars also from the contracts entered into A. D. 1450, for the fitting up of the Beauchamp Chapel, St. Mary's Church, Warwick. In the will of King Henry the Sixth, dated A. D. 1447, we find specific directions given for the size and arrangement of King's College Chapel, Cambridge; and no less than five different indentures are preserved, (the earliest dated A. D. 1513, the latest A. D. 1527,) containing contracts for the execution of different parts of that celebrated structure. The will of King Henry the Seventh, dated A. D. 1509, contains several orders and directions relating to the completion of the splendid chapel adjoining the abbey church, Westminster.

Q. Mention some of the earliest buildings of this style, the dates of the erection of which have been clearly ascertained?

A. The tower of St. Michael's Church, Coventry, the building of which commenced A. D. 1373 and was finished A. D. 1395140-*, is an early and fine specimen; the beautiful and lofty spire was, however, an after addition, like that at Salisbury Cathedral, and was not commenced till A. D. 1432. Westminster Hall140-†, the reparation or reconstruction of the greater part of which by King Richard the Second was commenced A. D. 1397 and finished A. D. 1399, has a fine groined porch, the front of which exhibits the square head over the arch of entrance; and the spandrels are filled with quatrefoils, inclosing shields and sunk panel-work. The large window above the porch, and that at the west end, are divided into panel-like compartments by vertical mullions, and a transom divides the principal lights horizontally. The wooden roof is of a more acute pitch than we usually find in buildings of this style, and is remarkable as a specimen of constructive art and display. The spaces between the arches and rafters are filled up to the ridge-piece with open panel-work ornamentally designed; and this is perhaps the earliest specimen we possess of the perpendicular wooden roof.

Q. What complete structures are there in this style of a late date, the periods of the erection of which are ascertained?

A. The design for the rebuilding of the Abbey Church, Bath, was planned and the reconstruction thereof commenced, by Bishop King, A. D. 1500; and after his death the works were carried on by Priors Bird and Hollowaye; but the church was not completed when the surrender of the monastery took place, A. D. 1539. The foundation of Henry the Seventh's Chapel, Westminster Abbey, was laid A. D. 1502, but the chapel was not completed till the reign of Henry the Eighth. It is the richest specimen, on a large scale, of this style of architecture, and is completely covered, both internally and externally, with panel-work, niches, statuary, heraldic devices, cognizances, and other decorative embellishment. The church at St. Neot's,

Huntingdonshire, is a fine large parochial edifice, all built apparently after one regular design, and consists of a tower covered with panel-work and ornament, with crocketed pinnacles at the angles and in front of each side; a nave, north and south aisles and chancel, and two chantry chapels, forming a continuation eastward of each aisle. It has a fine wooden roof, the cornice under which is in different parts curiously carved in relief. This church is said to have been erected A. D. 1507. But one of the most perfect specimens of a late date, on a smaller scale, is the church of Whiston, Northamptonshire, built A. D. 1534, by Anthony Catesby, esquire, lord of the manor, Isabel his wife, and John their son: it consists of a tower encircled with rows of quatrefoils and other decorative embellishment, and finished with crocketed pinnacles at the angles; a nave divided from the north and south aisles by arches within rectangular compartments, the spandrels of which are filled with sunk quatrefoils and foliated panels; these arches spring from piers disposed lozengewise with semicylindrical shafts at the angles; there are no clerestory windows, and the windows of the aisles and chancel have obtusely-pointed four-centred arches. The wooden roof is a good example of the kind.

St. Stephen's Church, Bristol.

Q. What district is noted for the number of rich churches in this style?

A. Somersetshire contains a number of fine churches, erected apparently towards the close of the fifteenth or very early in the sixteenth century; and many of these churches have much of carved woodwork in screens, rood-lofts, pulpits, and in pewing. The towers are, in particular, remarkable for their general style of design, and are often divided into stages by bands of quatrefoils; the sides are more or less ornamented with projecting canopied niches for statuary, and in many of these niches the statues have been preserved from the iconoclastic zeal which has elsewhere prevailed. The belfry windows are partly pierced, sometimes in quatrefoils, and partly filled with sunk panel-work. The parapets, whether embattled or straight-sided, are pierced with open work; and at each angle of the tower, at which buttresses are disposed rectangular-wise, is finished with a crocketed pinnacle, which is also often to be met with rising from the middle of the parapet. Towers similar in general design to those which may be said to prevail in Somersetshire are not unfrequently met with in other counties, but do not exhibit that provincialism which is the case in that particular county.

King Henry VII.'s Chapel, Westminster Abbey.

121-* Mr. Rickman, from whom this appellation is derived, has been since generally followed in his nomenclature.

137-* In Compton Church, Surrey, is, or until recently was, the remains of a wooden screen of late Norman character. Between the chancel and nave of Stanton Harcourt Church, Oxfordshire, is an early wooden screen in the style of the thirteenth century: the lower division is of plain panel-work, whilst the upper division consists of a series of open-pointed arches, trefoiled in the heads, and supported by slender cylindrical shafts with moulded bases and capitals, and an annulated moulding encircles each shaft midway up. In Northfleet Church, Kent, is a wooden screen which approximates in general design that at Stanton Harcourt, but is in a more advanced stage of art, being of the Early Decorated style: the lower portion of this is of plain panelling, while the open work forming the upper division above consists of a series of pointed arches, with tracery and foliations in and between the heads, supported by slender cylindrical shafts banded round midway with moulded bases and capitals, and these arches support a horizontal cornice. Specimens of decorated screen-work, some much mutilated, others in a more perfect state, are existing in the churches of King's Sutton, Northamptonshire; Croperdy, Oxfordshire; Beaudesert, Warwickshire; and in St. John's Church, Winchester. A characteristic distinction between screen-work of an earlier date than the fifteenth century and screen-work of that period will be found to consist in the slender cylindrical shafts, often annulated, sometimes not, with moulded bases and capitals which pertain to early work of the thirteenth and fourteenth centuries, and the mullion-like and angular-edged bars, often faced with small buttresses, which form the principal vertical divisions in screen-work of the fifteenth century.

140-* This stately monument of private munificence was erected at the sole charges of two brothers, Adam and William Botnor: it was twenty-one years in building, and cost each year 100*l.*

140-† Though not an ecclesiastical structure, it is here noticed as an example of the style in an early stage.

Window, Duffield Church, Derbyshire.

CHAPTER IX.

OF THE DEBASED ENGLISH STYLE.

Q. When did this style commence, and how long did it prevail or continue?

A. It may be said to have commenced about the year 1540, and to have continued to about the middle of the seventeenth century; but it is difficult to assign a precise date either for its introduction or discontinuance.

Q. Why is this style called the DEBASED?

A. From the general inferiority of design compared with the style it succeeded, from the meagre and clumsy execution of sculptured and other ornamental work, from the intermixture of detail founded on an entirely different school of art, and the consequent subversion of the purity of style.

Q. What may be considered as one great cause of this falling off?

A. The devastation of the monasteries, religious houses, and chantries, which followed their suppression, discouraged the study of ecclesiastical architecture, (which had been much followed by the members of the conventual foundations, who were now dispersed, in their seclusion,) and gave a fatal blow to that spirit of erecting and enriching churches which this country had for many ages possessed.

Q. How could this be the cause?

A. The expenses of erecting many of our ecclesiastical structures, or different portions of them, from time to time, in the most costly and beautiful manner, according to the style of the age in which such were built, were defrayed, some out of the immense revenues of the monasteries, which at their suppression were granted away by the crown, and others by the private munificence of individuals who frequently built an aisle, with a chantry chapel at the east end, partly inclosed by screen-work, or annexed to a church, a transept, or an additional chapel, endowed as a chantry, in order that remembrance might be specially and continually made of them in the offices of the church, according to the then prevailing usage; which chantries having been abolished, one motive for church-building was gone.

Q. What concurrent causes may also be assigned for this change?

A. The almost imperceptible introduction and advance, about this period, of a fantastic mode of architectural design and decoration, which is very apparent in the costly though in many respects inelegant monuments of this age, and in which details of ancient classic architecture were incorporated with others of fanciful design peculiar to the latter part of the sixteenth and early part of the seventeenth centuries.

Q. What are the characteristics of this style?

A. A general heaviness and inelegance of detail, doorways with pointed-arched heads exceedingly depressed in form, and also plain round-headed doorways, with key stones after the Roman or Italian semi-classic style now beginning to prevail; square-headed windows with plain vertical mullions, and the heads of the lights either round or obtusely arched, and generally without foliations; pointed windows clumsily formed, with plain mullion bars simply intersecting each other in the head, or filled with tracery miserably designed, and an almost total absence of ornamental mouldings. Indications of this style may be found in many country churches which have been repaired or partly rebuilt since the Reformation. In the interior of churches specimens of the wood-work of this style are very common, and may be perceived by the shallow and flat carved panelling, with round arches, arabesques, scroll-work, and other nondescript ornament peculiar to the age, with which the pews, reading-desks, and pulpits are often adorned. The screens of this period are constructed in a semi-classic style of design, with features and details of English growth, and are often surmounted with scroll-work, shields, and other accessories. Of this description of work the screen in the south aisle of Yarnton Church, Oxfordshire, constructed A. D. 1611, may be instanced as a curious specimen.

Arabesque.

Q. What peculiarity may be noted in the alterations and additions of this era?

A. A very common practice prevailed, from about the middle of the sixteenth century, when any alteration or addition was made in or to a church, of affixing a stone in the masonry, with the date of such in figures. Thus over the east window of Hillmorton Church, Warwickshire, (which is a pointed window of four lights, formed by three plain mullions curving and intersecting each other in the head, which is filled with nearly lozenge-shaped lights, but all without foliations,) is a stone bearing the date of 1640. In the south wall of the tower of the same church (which is low, heavy, and clumsily built, without any pretension to architectural design) is a stone to denote the period of its erection, which bears the date of 1655. Pulpits, communion-tables, church chests, poor-boxes, and pewing of the latter part of the sixteenth and of the seventeenth century, also very frequently exhibit, in figures carved on them, the precise periods of their construction.

Q. What specimens are there of this style of late or debased and mixed Gothic?

A. Annexed to Sunningwell Church, Berkshire, is a singular porch or building, sexagonal in form, at the angles of which are projecting columns of the Ionic order supporting an entablature. On each side of this building, except that by which it communicates with the church, and that in which the doorway is contained, is a plain window of the Debased Gothic style, of one light, with a square head and hood moulding over. The doorway is nondescript, neither Roman or Gothic. This building is supposed to have been erected by Bishop Jewell. The chapel of St. Peter's College, Cambridge, finished in 1632, exhibits in the east wall a large pointed window, clumsily designed, in the Debased style, and divided by mullions into five principal lights, round-headed, but trefoiled within; three series of smaller lights, rising one above the other, all of which are round-headed and trefoiled, fill the head of the window, the composition of which, though comparatively rude, is illustrative of the taste of the age. On each side of the window, on the exterior, is a kind of semi-classic niche. In Stowe Church, Northamptonshire, are a number of windows inserted at a general reparation of the church in 1639; these are square-headed, and have a label or hood moulding over, and are mostly divided into three obtusely pointed-arched lights, without foliations. Under the windows of the south aisle is a string-course, more of a semi-classic contour than Gothic. On the south side is a plain round-headed doorway, inserted at the same period. The tower and south aisle of Yarnton Church, Oxfordshire, erected by Sir Thomas Spencer, A. D. 1611, have the same kind of square-headed window, with arched lights without foliations, as those of Stow. Stanton-Harold Church, Leicestershire, erected A. D. 1653, is perhaps the latest complete specimen of the Debased Gothic style. Towards the end of this century Gothic mouldings appear not to have been understood, as in the attempt to reconstruct portions of churches in that style we find mouldings of classic art to prevail. Such is the case with respect to the tower of Eynesbury Church, St. Neot's, Huntingdonshire, rebuilt in a kind of Debased Gothic and mixed Roman style, in 1687. Other instances of the kind might also be enumerated. At the commencement of the eighteenth century the Roman or Italian mode appears to have prevailed generally in the churches then erected, without any admixture even of the Debased Gothic style.

Window, Ladbrook Church, Warwickshire.

Stoup, South Door, Oakham Church, Rutlandshire.

CONCLUDING CHAPTER.

ON THE INTERNAL ARRANGEMENT AND DECORATIONS OF A CHURCH.

THE churches of this country were anciently so constructed as to display, in their internal arrangement, certain appendages designed with architectonic skill, and adapted purposely for the celebration of mass and other religious offices.

At the Reformation, when the ritual was changed and many of the formularies of the church of Rome were discarded, some of such appendages were destroyed; whilst others, though suffered to exist, more or less in a mutilated condition, were no longer appropriated to the particular uses for which they had been originally designed.

On entering a church through the porch on the north or south side, or at the west end, we sometimes perceive on the right hand side of the door, at a convenient height from the ground, often beneath a niche, and partly projecting from the wall, a stone basin: this was the *stoup*, or receptacle for holy water, called also the *aspersorium*, into which each individual dipped his finger and crossed himself when passing the threshold of the sacred edifice. The custom of aspersion at the church door appears to have been derived from an ancient usage of the heathens, amongst whom, according to Sozomen154-*, the priest was accustomed to sprinkle such as entered into a temple with moist branches of olive. The stoup is sometimes found inside the church, close by the door; but the stone appendage appears to have been by no means general, and probably in most cases a movable vessel of metal was provided for the purpose; and in an inventory of ancient church goods at St. Dunstan's, Canterbury, taken A. D. 1500, we find mentioned "a stope off lede for the holy wat^r atte the church dore." We do not often find the stoup of so ancient a date as the twelfth century; one much mutilated, but apparently of that era, may however be met with inside the little Norman church of Beaudesert, Warwickshire, near to the south door.

The porch was often of a considerable size, and had frequently a groined ceiling, with an apartment above; it was anciently used for a variety of religious rites, for before the Reformation considerable portions of the marriage and baptismal services, and also much of that relating to the churching of women, were here performed, being commenced "ante ostium ecclesiæ," and concluded in the church; and these are set forth in the rubric of the Manual or service-book, according to the use of Sarum, containing those and other occasional offices.

Having entered the church, the font is generally discovered towards the west end of the nave, or north or south aisle, and near the principal door; such, at least, was in most cases its original and appropriate position: this was for the convenience of the sacramental rite there administered; part of the baptismal service (that of making the infant a catechumen) having been performed in the porch or outside the door156-*, he was introduced by the priest into the church, with the invitation, *Ingredere in templum Dei, ut habeas vitam æternam et vivas in sæcula sæculorum*; and after certain other rites and prayers the infant was carried to the font and immersed therein thrice by the priest, in the names of the three Persons of the Holy Trinity. By an ancient ecclesiastical constitution a font of stone or other durable material, with a fitting cover, was required to be placed in every church in which baptism could be administered156-†; and it was, as Lyndwood informs us, to be capacious enough for total immersion. Some ancient fonts are of lead, as that in Dorchester Church, Oxfordshire, and that in Childrey Church, Berkshire; both of these are cylindrical in shape, and of the Norman era, encircled with figures in relief; those on the font at Dorchester representing the twelve apostles, whilst those on that of Childrey are of bishops. Leaden fonts are also to be met with in the churches of Brookland, Kent; Wareham, Dorsetshire; and Walmsford, Northamptonshire. Square and cylindrical or truncated cone-like shaped fonts, of Norman design, supported on a basement by one or more shafts, and either plain or sculptured, are numerous; we sometimes find on them figures of the twelve apostles, sculptured in low relief; the baptism of our Saviour also was no uncommon representation. Fonts subsequent to the Norman era are not so frequently covered with sculptured figures, though such sometimes occur; they are sexagonal, septagonal, or octagonal in shape; and the different styles are easily ascertained by the architectural decorations, mouldings, tracery, and panel-work, with which they are more or less covered. On the sides of rich fonts of the fifteenth century representations of the seven sacraments were not unfrequently sculptured, as on that in Farningham Church, Kent. The covers to some rich fonts, especially to some of those of the fifteenth century, were very splendid, in shape somewhat resembling that of a spire, but the sides were covered with tabernacle-work, and decorated at the angles with small buttresses and crockets. Fonts with rich covers of this description are to be found in the churches of Ewelme, Oxfordshire; of North Walsham and of Worstead, Norfolk; and of Sudbury and of Ufford, Suffolk.158-*

The general situation of the tower or campanile is at the west end of the nave; it is sometimes, however, found in a different position, as at the west end of a side aisle, which is the case with respect to the churches of Monkskirby and Withybrooke, Warwickshire; or on one side of the church, as at Eynesbury Church, Huntingdonshire, and Alderbury Church, Salop; and the tower of the latter church is covered with what is called the saddle-back roof, having two gables—a peculiarity to be found in some few other churches. In cross churches the tower was generally, though not always, erected at the intersection of the transept, and between the nave and chancel. In the towers the church bells were hung, with the exception of one; without these no church was accounted complete; they were anciently consecrated with great ceremony, named and inscribed in honour of some saint, and the sound issuing from them was supposed to be of efficacy in averting the influence of evil spirits. Bells appear to have been introduced into this country in the latter part of the seventh century, but comparatively few bells are now remaining in our churches of an earlier date than the seventeenth century, since the commencement of which century most of our present church bells have been cast. Towers were also occasionally used, up to the fourteenth century, as parochial fortresses, to which in time of sudden and unforeseen danger the inhabitants of the parish resorted for awhile. The tower of Rugby Church, Warwickshire, a very singular structure built in the reign of Henry the Third, appears to have been erected for this purpose; it is of a square form, very lofty, and plain in construction, and is without a single buttress to support it; the lower windows are very narrow, and at a considerable distance from the ground; some of them are, in fact, mere loop-holes; the belfry windows are *square-headed*, of two lights, simply trefoiled in the head, and divided by a plain mullion; the only entrance was through the church; it has also a fire-place, the funnel for the conveyance of smoke being carried up through the thickness of the wall to a perforated battlement, and it altogether seems well calculated to resist a sudden attack. Other church towers of early date appear to have been erected for a double purpose: that of a campanile, as well as to afford temporary security. The towers of Newton Arlosh Church, of the Church of Burgh on the Sands, and of Great Salkeld Church, Cumberland, appear to have been constructed with a view to afford protection to the inhabitants of those villages upon any sudden invasion from the borders of Scotland, and for that purpose were strongly fortified160-*. Some church towers, especially in the counties of Norfolk and Suffolk, are round and batter, or gradually decrease in diameter as they rise upwards; most of these are of the Norman, though some are in the Early English, style; that at Little Saxham Church, Suffolk, may be adduced as a specimen. Spires in some instances appear to have served as landmarks, to guide travellers through woody districts and over barren downs. The spire of Astley Church, Warwickshire, now destroyed, was so conspicuous an object at a distance, that it was denominated the lantern of Arden. The spires of the churches of Monkskirby and Clifton, in the same county, now also destroyed, were formerly noticed as eminent landmarks.

Little Saxham Church Tower, Suffolk.

Open Seat, Culworth Church, Northamptonshire.

Anciently the body of the church appears to have contained no other fixed seats for the congregation than a solid mass of masonry raised against the wall, and forming a long stone bench or seat. A bench of this description runs along great part of the north, west, and south sides of the Norman church of Parranforth, Cornwall. In the Norman conventual church of Romsey plain stone benches of this description occur; they are likewise to be met with in Salisbury and other cathedrals; also in some of our ancient parish churches, as in the south aisle of Kidlington Church, Oxfordshire. Seats for the use of the congregation are noticed in the synod of Exeter, held A. D. 1287. Open wooden benches or pew-work are rarely, if at all, met with of an earlier era than the fifteenth century, when the practice of pewing the body of the church with open wooden seats, if not then introduced, began to prevail. In 1458 we meet with a testamentary bequest of money "to make seats called puying," and several of our churches still retain considerable remains of the ancient open seats of the fifteenth century. At Finedon, in Northamptonshire, the body of the church and aisles are almost entirely filled with low open seats, with carved tracery at the ends, disposed in four distinct rows; so that the whole of the congregation might sit facing the east. Similar seats occur in Culworth Church, in the same county, and these are likewise of the fifteenth century. The pulpit was anciently disposed towards the eastern part of the body of the church, but not in the centre of the aisle. Pulpits are now rarely to be found of an earlier date than the fifteenth century, when they appear to have been introduced into many churches, though not to have become a general appendage. Ancient pulpits of that era, whether of wood or stone, are covered with panel-work tracery and mouldings; and some exhibit signs of having been once elaborately painted and gilt. Mention, however, is made of pulpits at a much earlier period; for in the year 1187 one was set up in the abbey church, Bury St. Edmund's, from which, we are told, the abbot was accustomed to preach to the people in the vulgar tongue and provincial dialect164-*. The most ancient pulpit, perhaps, existing in this country, is that in the refectory of the abbey (now in ruins) of Beaulieu, Hampshire: it is of stone, and partly projects from the wall, and is ornamented with mouldings, sculptured foliage, and a series of blank trefoiled pointed arches, in the style of the thirteenth century. The church of the Holy Trinity, at Coventry, contains a fine specimen of a stone pulpit of the fifteenth century. In Rowington Church, in the county of Warwick, is a stone pulpit of the same age as that at Coventry, but much plainer in design. At Long Sutton Church, Somersetshire, is a splendid wooden pulpit of the fifteenth century, painted and gilt; and the sides are covered with ogee-headed niches, with angular-shaped buttresses between; but the pulpits of this era may be distinguished without difficulty by the peculiar architectural designs they exhibit.

We now approach the division between the nave or body of the church and the chancel or choir: this was formed by a beautiful and highly decorated screen, sometimes of stone, but generally of wood, panel and open-work tracery, painted and gilt: above this was a cross-beam, which formed a main support to the rood-loft, a gallery in which the crucifix or rood and the accompanying images of the blessed Virgin and St. John were placed so as to be seen by the parishioners in the body of the church, and also in accordance with the traditional belief that the position of our Saviour whilst suspended on the cross was facing the west. The passage to the rood-loft was generally up a flight of stone steps in the north or south wall of the nave; but as the rood-loft frequently extended across the aisles, we sometimes meet with a small turret annexed to the east end of one of the aisles for the approach. Though the introduction of the lattice-work division between the chancel and nave may be traced in the eastern church to the fourth century, we possess in our own churches few remains of screen-work of earlier date than the fifteenth century; and it appears probable that wooden screen-work before that period was not common, and that in most instances a curtain or veil was used for the purpose of division. The rood-loft generally projected in front, so as to form a kind of groined cove, the ribs of which sprang or diverged from the principal uprights of the screen beneath. In Long Sutton Church, Somersetshire, is a splendid wooden rood-loft, elaborately carved, painted, and gilt, which extends across the whole breadth of the church, and is approached by means of a staircase turret on the south side of the church. In the churches of Great Handborough, Enstone, Great Rollwright, and Hook Norton, Oxfordshire, are considerable remains of the ancient rood-loft, and numerous other instances where it is still retained could be adduced. Sometimes this gallery was so small as to admit of the rood and two attendant images only, and had no apparent access to it, as that in Wormleighton Church, Warwickshire. Hardly a rood-loft is, however, remaining of earlier date than the fifteenth century; prior to that period, and in many instances even during it, the crucifix or rood and its attendant images appear to have been affixed to a transverse beam extending horizontally across the chancel arch; this was sometimes richly carved, and a beam of this description still exists in the chancel of Little Malvern Church, Worcestershire. An earlier date than the eleventh century can hardly be assigned for the introduction of the rood, with the figures of St. Mary and St. John, into our churches, though in illuminated manuscripts somewhat before that period we find such figures pourtrayed with the crucifix[167-*]. In the abbey church, Bury St. Edmund's, the rood and the figures of St. Mary and St. John, which were placed over the high altar, were (as we are informed by Joceline, who wrote his Chronicle in the twelfth century) the gift of Archbishop Stigand[167-†]. Gervase, in describing the work of Lanfranc in Canterbury Cathedral, as it appeared before the fire, A. D. 1174, notices the rood-beam, which sustained a large crucifix and the images of St. Mary and St. John, as extended across the church between the nave and central tower[168-*].

Rood, Sherborne Church, Dorsetshire.

All the carved wooden roods appear to have been destroyed at the Reformation in compliance with the injunctions issued for that purpose. We occasionally meet, however, with bas relief sculptures of our Saviour extended on the cross, with a figure on each side representing the Virgin and St. John, but in a mutilated condition. On the outside of the west wall of the south transept of Romsey Church, Hants, and close to the entrance from the cloisters into the church, is a large stone rood or crucifix sculptured in relief, with a hand above emerging from a cloud169-*: this is apparently of the twelfth century. Small sculptured representations of the rood, with the figures of St. Mary and St. John, still exist on one of the buttresses near the west door of Sherborne Church, Dorsetshire; over a south doorway of Burford Church, Oxfordshire; and in the wall of the tower of the church of St. Lawrence, Evesham.

Sanctus Bell, Long Compton Church, Warwickshire.

Outside the roof of some churches, on the apex of the eastern gable of the nave, is a small open arch or turret, in which formerly a single bell was suspended: this was the *sanctus* or *sacringe* bell, thus placed that, being near the altar, it might be the more readily rung, when, in concluding the ordinary of the mass, the priest pronounced the *Ter-sanctus*, to draw attention to that more solemn office, the canon of the mass, which he was now about to commence; it was also rung at a subsequent part of the service, on the elevation and adoration of the host and chalice, after consecration171-*; but though the arch remains on the gable of the nave of many churches, the bell thus suspended is retained in few; amongst which may be mentioned those of Long Compton, Whichford, and Brailes, in Warwickshire, where this bell is still preserved hung in an arch at the apex of the nave, with the rope hanging down between the chancel and nave171-†. Mention of this bell is thus made in the Survey of the Priory of Sandwell, in the county of Stafford, taken at the time of the Reformation: "Itm the belframe standyng betw: the chauncell and the church, w^t. a litle *sanct^m* bell in the same." Generally, however, a small hand-bell was carried and rung at the proper times in the service, by the acolyte; and in inventories of ancient church furniture we find it often noticed as "*a sacringe bell;*" but in an inventory of goods belonging to the chapel of Thorp, Northamptonshire, it is described as "a litle *sanctus bell.*" A small sacringe bell, of bell-metal, with the exception of the clapper, which was of iron, was in 1819 discovered on the removal of some rubbish from the ruins of St. Margaret's Priory, Barnstable; and within the last few years a small sanctus bell was found on the site of a religious house at Warwick172-*.

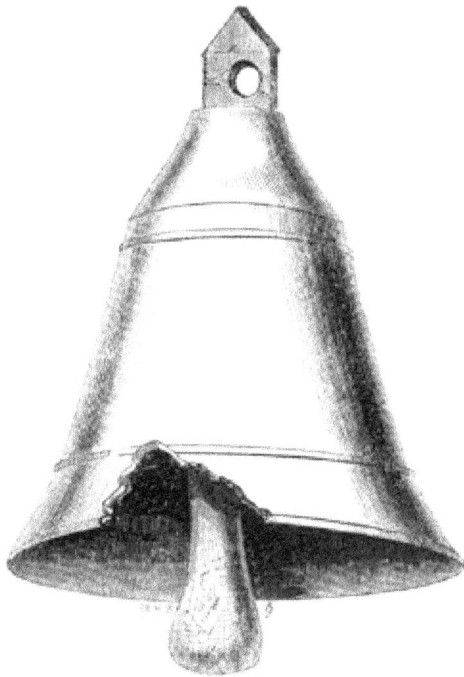

Ancient Sanctus Bell, found at Warwick.

Passing under the rood-loft, we enter the chancel: this was so called from the screen or lattice-work (cancelli) of stone or wood by which it was separated from the nave, and which succeeded the curtain or veil which anciently formed this division of the church173-*.

Stalls and Desk, St. Margaret's Church, Leicester.

We often perceive in the choirs of conventual churches, as in our cathedrals, on either side of the entrance, facing the east, and also on the north and south sides, a range of wooden stalls divided into single seats, peculiarly constructed, the *formulæ* or forms of which were movable, and carved on the *subselliæ* or under-sides with grotesque, satirical, and often irreverend devices: these were appropriated to the monks or canons of the monastery or college to which the church was attached. The form of each stall, when turned up so as to exhibit the carved work on the under-part, furnished a small kind of seat or ledge, constructed for the purpose of inclining against rather than sitting on; and this was called the *misericorde* or *miserere*. The *formulæ* or forms when down, and the misericordes when the forms were turned up, were used as the season required for penitential inclinations174-*. In front of these stalls was a desk, ornamented on the exterior with panelled tracery; and over the stalls, especially of those of cathedral churches, canopies of tabernacle work richly carved were sometimes disposed. In Winchester Cathedral we have perhaps the most early, chaste, and beautiful example of the canons' stalls, with canopies over, that are to be met with, although a greater excess of minute carved ornament may be found in the canopies which overhang the stalls in other cathedrals. In old conventual churches, now no longer used as such, the stalls have been often removed from their original position to other parts of the church, and they appear to have varied in number according to that of the fraternity.

Misericorde, All Souls' College, Oxford.

Brass Reading Desk, Merton College Chapel, Oxford.

In the choirs of cathedral and conventual churches, and in the chancels of some other churches, a movable desk, at which the epistle and gospel were read, was placed: this was often called the eagle desk, from its being frequently sustained on a brazen eagle with expanded wings, elevated on a stand, emblematic of St. John the evangelist. Eagle desks are generally found either of the fifteenth or seventeenth century; notices of them occur, however, much earlier. In the Louterell Psalter, written circa A. D. 1300, an eagle desk supported on a cylindrical shaft, banded midway down by an annulated moulding in the style of the thirteenth century, is represented; and in an account of ornaments belonging to Salisbury Cathedral, A. D. 1214, we find mentioned *Tuellia una ad Lectricum Aquilæ*. Besides the brass eagle desks which still remain in use in several of our cathedrals, and in the chapels of some of the colleges at Oxford and Cambridge, fine specimens are preserved in Redcliffe Church, Bristol, of the date 1638; in Croydon Church, Surrey; and in the church of the Holy Trinity at Coventry; other instances might also be enumerated. Sometimes we meet with ancient brass reading-desks which have not the eagle in front, but both the sides are sloped so as to form a double desk: of these, examples of the fifteenth century may be found in Yeovil Church, Somersetshire, and in the chapel of Merton College, Oxford. Ancient wooden reading-desks, either single or double, are also occasionally found; some of these are richly carved, others are comparatively plain, but all partake more or less of the architectonic style of the age in which they were severally constructed, and from which their probable dates may be ascertained. In Bury Church, Huntingdonshire, is a wooden desk with a single slope, and the vertical face presented in front is covered with arches and other carved ornaments: this perhaps may be referable to the latter part of the fourteenth century. A rich double desk, of somewhat later date, with the shaft supported by buttresses of open-work tracery, is preserved in Ramsey Church, Huntingdonshire. In Aldbury Church, Hertfordshire, is an ancient double lectern or reading desk, of wood, of the fifteenth century, much plainer in design than those at Bury and Ramsey; the shaft is angular, with small buttresses at the angles, and with a plain angular-shaped moulded capital and base, which latter is set on a cross-tree. In Hawstead Church, Suffolk, is a wooden desk with little ornament, supported on an angular shaft with an embattled capital, and moulded base with leaves carved in relief: this is apparently of the latter part of the fourteenth century. The ancient wooden desks found in some of our churches must not, however, be confounded with a more numerous class constructed and used subsequent to the Reformation.

Proceeding up the chancel or choir, we ascend by three steps to the platform, on which the high altar anciently stood: this was so called to distinguish it from other altars, of which there were often several, in the same church; high mass was celebrated at it, whereas the other altars were chiefly used for the performance of low or private masses. The most ancient altars were of wood, afterwards they were constructed of stone; those of the primitive British churches are spoken of by St. Chrysostom. By a decree of the council of Paris, held A. D. 509, no altar was to be built but of stone. Amongst the excerptions of Ecgbert, archbishop of York A. D. 750, was one that no altars should be consecrated with chrism but such as were made of stone; and by the council of Winchester, held under Lanfranc A. D. 1076, altars were enjoined to be of stone. The customary form of such was a mass of stone supporting an altar table or slab, and resembling the tombs of the martyrs, at which the primitive Christians held their meetings; from which circumstance it became customary to enclose in every altar relics of some saint, and without such relics an altar was esteemed incomplete.

Ancient Pix, Ashmolean Museum, Oxford.

Pertaining to the high altar, which was covered with a frontal and cloths, and anciently enclosed at the sides with curtains suspended on rods of iron projecting from the wall, was a crucifix, which succeeded to the simple cross placed on the altars of the Anglo-Saxon churches; a pair180-* of candlesticks, generally with spikes instead of sockets, on which lights or tapers were fixed; a pix, in which the host was kept reserved for the sick; a pair of cruets, of metal, in which were contained the wine and water preparatory to their admixture in the eucharistic cup; a sacring bell; a pax table, of silver or other metal, for the kiss of peace, which took place shortly before the host was received in communion; a stoup or stok, of metal, with a sprinkle for holy water; a censer or thurible181-*, and a ship, (a vessel so called,) to hold frankincense; a chrismatory181-†, an offering basin, a basin which was used when the priest washed his hands, and a chalice and paten. Costly specimens of the ancient pix, containing small patens for the reception of the host, are preserved amongst the plate belonging to New College and Corpus Christi College, Oxford. A pix of a much plainer description, but without its cover, of the metal called latten, was until recently preserved in the church of Enstone, Oxfordshire: the body of this was of a semi-globular form, supported on an angular stem, with a knob in the midst, and in appearance not unlike a chalice. The monstrance, in which the host was exhibited to the people, and which has been sometimes confounded with the pix182-*, does not appear to have been introduced into our churches before the fifteenth century; on the suppression of the monasteries and chantries we find it noticed in the inventories then taken of church furniture, as in that of the Priory of Ely, where it is called "a stonding monstral for the sacrament;" and in that of St. Augustine's Monastery, Canterbury, where it is described as "one monstrance, silver gilt, with four glasses."

Sedilia, Crick Church, Northamptonshire.

Near the high altar we frequently find, in the south wall of the chancel, a series of stone seats, sometimes without but generally beneath plain or enriched arched canopies, often supported by slender piers which serve to divide the seats. In most instances these seats are three in number, but they vary from one to five, and are the *sedilia* or seats formerly appropriated during high mass to the use of the officiating priest and his attendant ministers, the deacon and sub-deacon, who retired thither during the chanting of the *Gloria in excelsis*, and some other parts of the service183-*. The sedilia sometimes preserve the same level, but generally they graduate or rise one above another, and that nearest the altar, being the highest, was occupied by the priest; the other two by the deacon and sub-deacon in succession183-†. We do not often meet with sedilia of so early an era as the twelfth century; there are, however, instances of such, as in the church of St. Mary, at Leicester, where is a fine Norman triple sedile, divided into graduating seats by double cylindrical piers with sculptured capitals, and the recessed arches they support are enriched on the face with a profusion of the zigzag moulding. In the south wall of the choir of Broadwater Church, Sussex, is a stone bench beneath a large semicircular Norman arch, the face of which is enriched with the chevron or zigzag moulding. In Avington Church, Berkshire, is a stone beneath a plain segmental arch. Norman sedilia also occur in the churches of Earls Barton, Northamptonshire, and of Wellingore, Lincolnshire. From the commencement of the thirteenth century up to the Reformation sedilia became a common appendage to a church, and the styles are easily distinguished by their peculiar architectonic features. Some are without canopies, and are excessively plain. On the south side of the chancel of Minster Lovel Church, Oxfordshire, is a stone bench without a canopy or division, and plain stone benches thus disposed are found in the chancel of Bloxham Church, Oxfordshire, and of Rowington Church, Warwickshire. In Sedgeberrow Church, Gloucestershire, are two sedilia without canopies; and in Standlake Church, Oxfordshire, the sedilia, three in number, are without canopies or ornament. In Spratten Church, Northamptonshire, is a stone bench for three persons under a plain recessed pointed arch. In Priors Hardwick Church, Warwickshire, is a sedile for the priest, and below that one double the size for the deacon and sub-deacon; both are under recessed arched canopies. Quadruple sedilia occur in the churches of Turvey and Luton, Bedfordshire; in the Mayor's Chapel, Bristol; in Gloucester Cathedral; in the church of Stratford-upon-Avon, Warwickshire; and in Rothwell Church, Northamptonshire: these are beneath canopies, and most of them are highly enriched. Quintuple sedilia sometimes occur, but are very rare; in the conventual church of Southwell, Nottinghamshire, are, however, five sedilia beneath ogee-headed canopies richly ornamented. A single sedile for one person only is occasionally met with, but not often.

Double Piscina, Salisbury Cathedral.

Eastward of the sedilia, in the same wall, is a *fenestella* or niche, sometimes plain, but often enriched with a crocketed ogee or pedimental hood moulding in front, over the arch, which is trefoiled or cinquefoiled in the head. This niche contains a hollow perforated basin or stone drain, called the *piscina* or *lavacrum*186-*, into which it appears that after the priest had washed his hands, which he was accustomed to do before the consecration of the elements and again after the communion, the water was poured, as also that with which the chalice was rinsed. The usage of washing the hands before the communion is one of very high antiquity, and is expressly noticed in the Clementine Liturgy, and by St. Cyril in his mystical Catechesis187-*; we do not, however, find the piscina in our churches of an era earlier than the twelfth century, and even then it was of uncommon occurrence; but in the thirteenth century the general introduction is observable. In Romsey Church, Hampshire, is the shaft and basin (the latter cushion-shaped) of a curious Norman piscina: this is now lying loose, in a dilapidated state. In the south apsis of the same church is another Norman piscina, consisting of a quadrangular-shaped basin projecting from the south wall; and on the south side of the chancel of Avington Church, Berkshire, is a plain Norman piscina within a simple semicircular arched recess. The churches of Kilpeck, Herefordshire, Keelby, Lincolnshire, and Bapchild, Kent, also contain Norman piscinæ. Those of all the various styles of later date are common; they exhibit, however, an interesting variety in design and ornamental detail. The drain of the piscina communicated with a perforated stone shaft, commonly enclosed in the wall, through which the water was lost in the earth; as in the case of the piscina with its shaft taken out of the south wall of the chancel of the now destroyed church of Newnham Regis, Warwickshire. Sometimes a piscina was a subsequent addition to a structure of early date, as in the old and now demolished church of Stretton-upon-Dunsmore, Warwickshire, in the south wall of the Norman chancel of which a piscina of the latter part of the thirteenth century had been inserted.

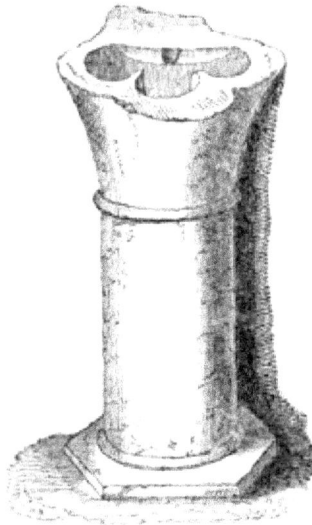

Piscina, Newnham Regis, Warwickshire.

The piscina is very common in churches even where the sedilia or stone seats are wanting, and not only in the chancel, but also in the south walls at the east end of the north and south aisles, and in mortuary chapels, as will be presently noticed; it appears, in short, to have been an indispensable appendage to an altar.

Sometimes the piscina is double, and contains two basins with drains, the one for receiving the water in which the hands had been washed, the other for the reception of the water with which the chalice was rinsed after the communion189-*. In Rothwell Church, Northamptonshire, on the south side of the chancel, are the vestiges of a triple piscina; the fenestella has been destroyed, but the three basins with their drains remain.

Across the *fenestella*, or niche which contains the piscina, a shelf of stone or wood may be frequently found: this was the *credence*190-*, or table on which the chalice, paten, ampullæ, and other things necessary for the celebration of mass were, before consecration, placed in a state of readiness on a clean linen cloth; and this originated from the πρόθεσις, or side table of preparation, used in the early church; a recurrence to which ancient and primitive custom by some of the divines of the Anglican church, after the

Reformation, occasioned great offence to be taken by the Puritan seceders. In some instances a side table of stone or wood was used for this purpose; and a fine credence table of stone, the sides of which are covered with panelled compartments, is still remaining on the south side of the choir, St. Cross Church, near Winchester190-†.

Ambrie or Locker, Chaddesden Church, Derbyshire.

The credence table, or shelf above the piscina, must not be confounded with the *ambrie* or *locker*, a small square and plain recess usually contained in the east or north wall, near the altar. In this the chalice, paten, and other articles pertaining to the altar were kept when not in use. The wooden doors formerly affixed to these ambries have for the most part either fallen into decay or been removed, but traces of the hinges may be frequently perceived; and a locker in the north wall of the chancel of Aston Church, Northamptonshire, still retains the two-leaved wooden door. Sometimes shelves are set across the lockers. In the east wall of Earls Barton Church, Northamptonshire, is a large locker divided into two unequal parts by a stone shelf inserted in it; and in the north aisle of Salisbury Cathedral are two large triangular-headed lockers or ambries, each which contains two shelves.

Within the north wall of the chancel, near the altar, a large arch, like that of a tomb, may often be perceived; within this the *holy sepulchre*, generally a wooden and movable structure, was set up at Easter, when certain rites commemorative of the burial and resurrection of our Lord were anciently performed with great solemnity; for on Good Friday the crucifix and host were here deposited, and watched the following day and nights; and early on Easter morning they were removed from thence with great ceremony, and replaced on the altar by the priest. In the accounts of churchwardens of the fifteenth and early part of the sixteenth century we meet with frequent notices of payments made for watching the sepulchre at Easter192-*. Sometimes the sepulchre was altogether of stone, and a fixture, and enriched with architectural and sculptured detail, as in the well-known specimen at Heckington, Lincolnshire, and the fine specimen of tabernacle-work in Stanton Harcourt Church, Oxfordshire.

At the back of the high altar was affixed a reredos, or screen of tabernacle-work, costly specimens of which contained small images set on brackets under projecting canopies; an alabaster table or sculptured bas relief, placed just over the altar, was also common. The high altar reredos is still remaining, though in a mutilated condition, in the Abbey Church, St. Alban's; it was erected A. D. 1480, and is perhaps the most splendid specimen we have; and in Bristol Cathedral a portion of the high altar reredos is also left. The chantry altar reredos is more frequently remaining, even where the altar and alabaster table193-* above have been destroyed; rarely, however, in a perfect state. In the seventeenth century the rich tabernacle-work was sometimes plastered over, probably to preserve it from iconoclastic violence. In many of our cathedrals, as at Gloucester, Bristol, Wells, and Worcester, and in some of the chantries attached to Henry the Seventh's Chapel, Westminster, specimens of the chantry reredos screen, which appear to have abounded more or less with sculptured and architectural detail, are to be met with; and remains of the painting and gilding with which they were anciently covered may in some instances be traced. In a Survey of the Priory Church, Bridlington, taken at the suppression, we find noticed, "The Reredose at the highe alter representyng Criste at the assumpcyon of our Lady and the XII. appostells, w^t. dyvers other great imagys, beyng of a great heyght, ys excellently well wrought, and as well gylted." Five small chapels are also mentioned, "w^t. fyve alters and small tables of alleblaster and imag's." Sometimes, however, the space behind the altar was occupied by a painted altar-piece, on wood or panel; a curious but mutilated specimen of which, of the latter part of the fifteenth century, is still preserved in the conventual church, Romsey.

Over the high altar was the great east window of the church, glazed with painted glass; other windows in the church were also thus filled. The subjects pourtrayed on the glass were sometimes scriptural, sometimes legendary. Single figures of saints, distinguished by their peculiar symbols, are common; figures of crowned heads, prelates, and warriors also frequently occur; and on some windows are depicted the arms and sometimes even the portraits of different benefactors to the church, with scrolls bearing inscriptions. We have, perhaps, few remains of ancient stained glass in our churches of a period antecedent to the thirteenth century: of this era, probably, are those curious circular designs which fill the greater portion of the lights at the back of the sedilia in Dorchester Church, Oxfordshire: one representing St. Augustine and St. Birinus, the first bishop of that ancient see; another, a priest and deacon, the former with the host, the latter bearing the ampullæ. Of this period also is some ancient stained glass in Chetwood Church, Bucks, the ground of which is covered with a kind of mosaic pattern, a usual feature in the more ancient stained glass, and the borders partake of a tendril foliage; whilst in pointed oval-shaped compartments, forming the well-known symbol *vesica piscis*, are single figures of saints and crowned heads, each clad in a vest and mantle of two different colours. In the fourteenth century single figures under rich canopies are common, but we begin to lose sight of the mosaic pattern as a back-ground. The stained glass in the windows of the choir of Merton College Chapel, Oxford, is either very early in this, or of a late period in the preceding century, and exhibits single figures under rich canopies: over the head of one of these, (the kneeling figure of a monk in his cowl,) is a scroll inscribed "*Magister Henricus de Mammesfeld me fecit.*" In the windows of Tewkesbury Abbey Church are several single figures of this period, some of knights in armour. In the chancel of Stanford Church, Northamptonshire, are single figures of the apostles in painted glass, each appearing within an ogee-headed canopy, cinquefoiled within the head and crocketed externally, and the sides of the canopy are flanked by pinnacled buttresses in stages. Specimens of stained glass of the fifteenth century are numerous in comparison with those of an earlier period; we find such in the east window of Langport Church, Somersetshire, where single figures occur of St. Clemens, St. Catherine, St. Elizabeth, and of many other saints. Some splendid remains of painted glass of the fifteenth century are likewise preserved in the windows of the choir of Ludlow Church, Salop, mostly in single figures; amongst them is the representation of St. George in armour, of the reign of Henry the Seventh; the figures of the Virgin and infant Christ may also be noticed. Towards the close of this century kneeling figures, not merely disposed single, but also in groups, formally arranged, may be observed. As a composition, wherein a better display of grouping and aerial perspective is evinced, the splendid window in St. Margaret's Church, Westminster, of the crucifixion between the two thieves, and numerous figures in the foreground, not grouped formally but with artistical feeling, with the figures of St. George and St. Catherine on each side of the principal design, and the portraits of Henry the Seventh and his consort Elizabeth in separate compartments beneath, each kneeling before a faldstool, may be noticed. This window, which in some of the details exhibits an approach to the renaissance style, was presented to Henry the

Seventh by the magistrates of Dort in Holland, to adorn his chapel at Westminster. The era of the various specimens of ancient stained glass we meet with in our churches may generally be ascertained by the costume and disposition of the figures, the form of the shields, the mosaic pattern or other back-ground, and architectural designs of the canopies.

The pavement beneath the high altar was frequently composed of small square encaustic bricks or tiles, whereon the arms of founders and benefactors, interspersed with figures, flowers, and emblematic devices, were impressed, painted, and glazed; other parts of the church were also paved with these tiles.

The walls of the church were covered with fresco paintings of the day of judgment, legendary stories, portraits of saints, and scriptural, allegorical, and historical subjects, in the conventional styles of the different ages in which such were executed, the costume and details being according to the fashion then prevailing. These paintings have in most churches been obliterated by repeated coats of whitewash, so that few perfect specimens now remain; traces of such are, however, occasionally brought to light in the alteration and reparation of our ancient churches. The subject of the judgment-day was commonly represented on the west wall of the nave, or over the chancel arch; and in the contract for the erection of the Lady Chapel, St. Mary's Church, Warwick, A. D. 1454, is a covenant "to paint fine and curiously, to make on the west wall the dome of our Lord God Jesus, and all manner of devises and imagery thereto belonging." The west front of the wall over the chancel arch, Trinity Chapel, Stratford-upon-Avon, was some years back found to be thus covered; but this painting, with others in the same chapel, was afterwards again obliterated199-*. A curious fresco painting of the last judgment, discovered a few years ago on the west face of the wall over the chancel arch, Trinity Church, Coventry, has, however, been very carefully preserved, and the coat of whitewash which tended to conceal it probably ever since the Reformation has been judiciously removed. The legend of St. Christopher, represented by a colossal figure with a beam-like walking-staff, carrying the infant Christ on his shoulders through the water, was generally painted on the north wall of the nave or body of the church. A fresco painting of this subject, half obliterated, is still apparent on the north wall of the nave of Burford Church, Oxfordshire; and other instances might be adduced. The murder of Archbishop Becket was also a very favourite subject: an early pictorial representation of the thirteenth century, of this event, is still visible on one of the walls of Preston Church, Sussex; it formed, likewise, one of the subjects represented on the walls of Trinity Chapel, Stratford-upon-Avon; and a painting of the same subject on panel, executed in the middle of the fifteenth century, was formerly suspended over or near the tomb of Henry the Fourth in Canterbury Cathedral200-*. Several vestiges of ancient fresco wall-paintings, more or less obliterated, are still preserved in Winchester Cathedral. The walls of our churches were even in the Anglo-Saxon era embellished with paintings; and such are described as decorating the walls of the church of Hexham in the seventh century. By the synod of Calcuith, held A. D. 816, a representation of the saint to whom a church was dedicated was required to be painted either on the wall of the church or on a tablet suspended in the church.

Ancient Stone Reliquary or Shrine, Brixworth Church, Northamptonshire.

In most of the large conventual churches, and also in some of the smaller parochial churches, shrines containing relics of the patron or other saints were exhibited; these were either fixed and immovable, of tabernacle-work, of stone or wood, or partly of both, or were small movable feretories, which could be carried on festivals in procession. Of the fixed shrines, that in Hereford Cathedral of Bishop Cantelupe, of the date A. D. 1287, is a fine and early specimen, in very fair preservation. In the north aisle of the abbey church, Shrewsbury, are some remains of a stone shrine, which from the workmanship may be considered as a production of the early part of the fifteenth century: this is much mutilated: but the shrine of St. Frideswide, in Oxford Cathedral, the lower part of which is composed of a stone tomb, the upper part of rich tabernacle-work of wood, is still tolerably perfect: this is also of the fifteenth century. Of the small movable feretories, one apparently of the workmanship of the twelfth century, seven inches long and six high, formed of wood, enamelled and gilt, with figures on the sides representing the crucifixion, is still preserved in Shipley Church, Sussex; and a small stone reliquary or shrine of the fourteenth century was discovered a few years ago, and is now preserved in the church of Brixworth, Northamptonshire.

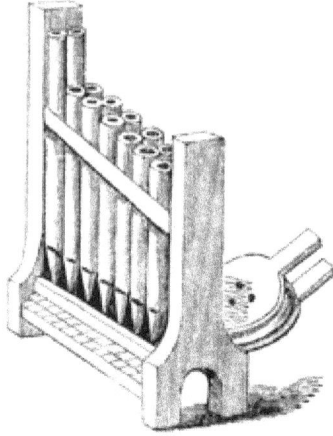

Ancient Organ.

The organ, as a solemn musical instrument, may claim a very early origin, and has been in use in our churches from the Anglo-Saxon era. The ancient organs were small, and all the pipes were exposed. The phrase "*a pair of organs*," so frequently met with in old inventories and church accounts, may probably have answered to the great and choir organ of a subsequent period—one instrument in two divisions. The mechanism of the old organs was rude and simple, compared with the improvements of modern times, and the cost was small; they were generally placed in the rood-loft.

The church chest is often an ancient and interesting object: sometimes we find it rudely formed, or hollowed out of the solid trunk of a tree, with a plain or barrel-shaped lid of considerable thickness. The churches of Bradford Abbas, Dorsetshire; Long Sutton, Somersetshire; and Ensham, Oxfordshire; contain chests thus rudely constructed. Sometimes they are strongly banded about with iron. The fronts and sides of these chests are not unfrequently embellished more or less richly with carved tracery, panel-work, and other detail in the style prevalent at the period of their construction. In Clemping Church, Sussex, is an early chest of the thirteenth century, the front of which exhibits a series of plain pointed arches trefoiled in the head, and other carved work. In Haconby Church, Lincolnshire, and in Chevington Church, Suffolk, are very rich chests covered with tracery and detail in the decorated style of the fourteenth century. In Brailes Church, Warwickshire, is an ancient chest of the fifteenth century covered with panel-work compartments, with plain pointed arches foliated in the heads. Panelled chests of this century are numerous. In Shanklin Church, Isle of Wight, is a chest bearing the date of 1519, on which no architectural ornament is displayed, but the initials T. S. (Thomas Selkstead) are fancifully designed, and are separated by the lock, and a coat of arms beneath.

In the south wall of each aisle, near the east end, and also in other parts of the church, we frequently find the same kind of fenestella or niche containing a piscina, and sometimes a credence shelf, as that before described as being in the chancel: this is a plain indication that an altar has been erected in this part of the church; and this end of the aisle was generally separated from the rest of the church by a screen, the lower part of panel, the upper part of open-work tracery, of stone or wood, similar to that forming the division between the chancel and nave; and the space thus enclosed was converted into or became a private chapel or chantry; for it was anciently the custom, especially during the fourteenth and fifteenth centuries, for lords of manors and persons of wealth and local importance to build or annex small chapels or side aisles to their parish churches, and these were endowed by license from the crown with land sufficient for the maintenance, either wholly or in part, of one or more priests, who were to celebrate private masses daily or otherwise, as the endowment expressed, at the altar erected therein, and dedicated to some saint, for the souls of the founder, his ancestors and posterity, for whose remains these chantry chapels frequently served as burial-places. At this service, however, no congregation was required to be present, but merely the priest, and an acolyte to assist him; and it was in allusion to the low or private masses thus performed, that Bishop Jewell, whilst condemning the practice as untenable, observes, "And even suche be their private masses, for the most part sayde in side iles, alone, without companye of people, onely with one boye to make answer."

The screens by which these chapels were enclosed have in numerous instances been destroyed; still many have been preserved, and chantry chapels parted off the church by screen-work of stone may be found in the churches of Bradford Abbas, Dorsetshire; and Aldbury, Hertfordshire; in which latter church is a very perfect specimen of a mortuary chapel, with a monument and recumbent effigies in the midst of it. Chantry chapels enclosed on two of the sides by wooden screen-work are more common.

Although no ancient high altar of stone is known to exist, some of the ancient chantry altars have been preserved: these are composed either of a solid mass of masonry, covered with a thick slab or table of stone, as in the north aisle of Bengeworth Church, near Evesham, and in the south aisle of Enstone Church, Oxfordshire; or of a thick stone slab or table, with a cross at each angle and in the centre, supported merely on brackets or trusses built into and projecting from the wall, as in a chantry chapel in Warmington Church, Warwickshire; or partly on brackets and partly sustained on shafts or slender piers, as in a chantry chapel, Chipping-Norton Church, Oxfordshire. Sometimes a chamber containing a fire-place was constructed over a chantry, apparently for the residence, either occasional or permanent, of a priest: such a chamber occurs over the chantry chapel containing the altar in Chipping-Norton Church; and such also, with the exception of the flooring, which has decayed or been removed, may be seen in the chantry chapel which contains the altar in Warmington Church. In both of these chambers are windows or apertures in the walls which divide them from the church, through which the priest was enabled to observe unseen any thing passing within the church.

Chantry Altar, Warmington Church, Warwickshire

We often find an opening or aperture obliquely disposed, carried through the thickness of the wall at the north-east angle of the south, and the south-east angle of the north aisle: this was the *hagioscope*, through which at high mass the elevation of the host at the high altar, and other ceremonies, might be viewed from the chantry chapel situate at the east end of each aisle. In general, these apertures are mere narrow oblong slits; sometimes, however, they partake of a more ornamental character, as in a chantry chapel on the south side of Irthlingborough Church, Northamptonshire, where the head of an aperture of this kind is arched, cinquefoiled within, and finished above with an embattled moulding. In the north and south transepts of Minster Lovel Church, Oxfordshire, are oblique openings, arched-headed and foliated; and in the north aisle of Chipping-Norton Church, in the same county, is a singular hagioscope, obliquely disposed, not unlike a square-headed window of three foliated arched lights, with a quatrefoil beneath each light.

We sometimes meet with one or more brackets, with plain mouldings or sculptured, projecting from the east wall of a chancel aisle or chantry chapel; and on these, lamps or lights were formerly set, and kept continually burning in honour of the Virgin or of some other saint; and we also meet with rich projecting canopies or recessed niches, with brackets beneath, on which images of saints were formerly placed.

The use of the low side window, common in some districts, near the south-west angle of the chancel, and sometimes, but not so frequently, near the north-west angle, and occasionally even in the aisle, has not been correctly ascertained; it has, however, been conjectured to have served for the purpose of a confessional; and on minute examination indications of its formerly having had a wooden shutter, which opened on the inside, are sometimes visible; and on the south side of Kenilworth Church, Warwickshire, is an iron-barred window of this description, on which the wooden shutter is still retained.209-*

The sedilia or stone seats, so frequently found in the south wall of the chancel, are occasionally, though not often, to be met with in the south walls of side aisles or chantry chapels: when this is the case it is presumed the endowment was for more priests than one.

Such, not to digress into more minute particulars, may suffice to convey a general idea of the manner in which our churches were internally decorated, and how they were fitted up, with reference to the ceremonial rites of the church of Rome, in and before the year 1535. The walls were covered with fresco paintings, the windows were glazed with stained glass; the rood-loft and the pulpit, where the latter existed, were richly carved, painted, and gilt; and the altars were garnished with plate and sumptuous hangings. Altar-tombs with cumbent effigies were painted so as to correspond in tone with the colours displayed on the walls; the pavement of encaustic tiles, of different devices, was interspersed with sepulchral slabs and inlaid brasses; and screen-work, niches for statuary, mouldings, and sculpture of different degrees of excellence, abounded. Suspended from aloft hung the funeral achievement; at a later period, even more common, the banner, helme, crest, gauntlets, spurs, sword, targe, and cote armour.210-* In addition to these were, in some churches, shrines and reliquaries, enriched by the lavish donations of devotees, and wooden images excessively decked out and appareled211-*—objects of superstition, to which pilgrimages and offerings were made. And if in the review of the conceptions of a prior age, viz. of the fourteenth century, we find a higher rank of art to be evinced, and the style and combination of architectural and sculptured detail to be more severe and pure, at no period were our churches adorned to greater excess than on the eve of that in which all were about to undergo spoliation, and many of them wanton destruction.

For on the suppression of the monasteries and colleges, to the number of 700 and upwards, and of the chantries, in number more than 2300, effected between the years 1535 and 1540, the abbey churches were not only despoiled of their costly vestments, altar plate and furniture, and shrines enriched with silver, gold, and jewels, but many of them were entirely dismantled, and the sites with the materials granted to individuals by whom they were soon reduced to a state of ruin. Some were even, either then or in after-times, converted into dwelling-houses; and others, or some portion of such, were allowed to be preserved as parochial churches; but the private chantry altars, though left bare and forsaken, were not as yet ordered to be destroyed.

By the royal injunctions exhibited A. D. 1538, such feigned images as were known to be abused of pilgrimages, or offerings of any kind made thereunto, were, for the avoiding of idolatry, to be forthwith taken down without delay, and no candles, tapers, or images of wax were from thenceforth to be set before any image or picture, "but onelie the light that commonlie goeth about the crosse of the church by the rood-loft, the light afore the sacrament of the altar, and the light about the sepulchre;" which, for the adorning of the church and divine service, were for the present suffered to remain. By the same injunctions a Bible of the largest volume, in English, was directed to be set up in some convenient place in every church, that the parishioners might resort to the same and read it; and a register-book was ordered to be kept, for the recording of christenings, marriages, and burials.

But beyond the suppression of the monasteries and chantries, an act the effect of secular rather than religious motives, little alteration was made during the reign of Henry the Eighth in the ceremonies and services of the church, although the minds of many were becoming prepared for the change which afterwards ensued. And in the reign of his successor, Edward the Sixth, a striking difference was effected in the internal appearance of our churches; for many appendages were, not all at once, but by degrees, and under the authority of successive injunctions, discarded. Thus, by the king's injunctions published in 1547, all images which had been abused with pilgrimage, or offering of any thing made thereunto, were, for the avoiding of the detestable offence of idolatry, by ecclesiastical authority, but not by that of private persons, to be taken down and destroyed; and no torches or candles, tapers or images of wax, were to be thenceforth suffered to be set before any image or picture, "but only two lights upon the high altar before the sacrament, which, for the signification that Christ is the very true light of the world, they shall suffer to remain still." And as to such images which had not been abused, and which as yet were suffered to remain, the parishioners were to be admonished by the clergy that they served for no other purpose but to be a remembrance. The Bible in English, and the Paraphrases of Erasmus upon the Gospels, also in English, were ordered to be provided and set up in every church for the use of the parishioners. It was also enjoined that at every high mass the gospel and epistle should be read in English, and not in Latin, in the pulpit or in some other convenient place, so that the people might hear the same. Processions about the church and churchyard were now ordered to be disused, and the priests and clerks were to kneel in the midst of the church immediately before high mass, and there sing or read the Litany in English set forth by the authority of King Henry the Eighth. By the same injunctions all shrines, covering of shrines, all tables, candlesticks, trindles or rolls of wax, pictures, paintings, and all other monuments of feigned miracles, pilgrimages, idolatry, and superstition, were directed to be utterly taken away and destroyed; so that there should remain no memory of the same in walls, glass windows, or elsewhere within churches; and in every church "a comely and honest pulpit" was to be provided at the cost of the parishioners, to be set in a convenient place for the preaching of God's word; and a strong chest, having three keys, with a hole in the upper part thereof, was to be set and fastened near unto the high altar, to the intent the parishioners should put into it their oblation and alms for their poor neighbours215-*.

Hence the primary introduction of desks with divinity books, the litany stool, and the charity box, yet retained in some of our churches. But as much contention arose respecting the taking down of images, also as to whether they had been idolatrously abused or not, all images without exception were shortly afterwards, by royal authority, ordered to be removed and taken away.

In the ritual the first formal change appears to have been the order of the communion set forth in 1547 as a temporary measure only, until other order should be provided for the true and right manner of administering the sacrament according to the rule of the scriptures of God, and first usage of the primitive church. In this the term *altar* is alone made use of; but in the first Liturgy of King Edward the Sixth, published in 1549, the altar or table whereupon the Lord's Supper was ministered is indifferently called *the altar, the Lord's table, God's board.* Ridley, bishop of London, by his diocesan injunctions issued in 1550, after noticing that in divers places some used the Lord's board after the form of a table, and some as an altar, exhorted the curates, churchwardens, and questmen to erect and set up the Lord's board after the form of an honest table, decently covered, in such place of the quire or chancel as should be thought most meet, so that the ministers with the communicants might have their place separated from the rest of the people; and to take down and abolish all other by-altars or tables. Soon after this, orders of council were sent to the bishops, in which, after noticing that the altars in most churches of the realm had been taken down, but that there yet remained altars standing in divers other churches, by occasion whereof much variance and contention arose, they were commanded, for the avoiding of all matters of further contention and strife about the standing or taking away of the said altars216-*, to give substantial order that all the altars in every church should be taken down, and instead of them that a table should be set up in some convenient part of the chancel, to serve for the ministration of the blessed communion; and reasons were at the same time published why the Lord's board should rather be after the form of a table than of an altar, expressing however in what sense it might be called an altar. In the second Liturgy of King Edward the Sixth, amongst other important changes both of doctrine and discipline, the word *altar*, as denoting the communion-table, was purposely omitted.

The peculiar formation, frequently observable, of the old communion-tables, seems to have originated from the diversity of opinion held by many in the Anglican church, as to whether or not there was in the sacrament of the Lord's Supper a memorative sacrifice; for by those who held the negative they were so constructed, not merely that they might be moved from one part of the church to another, but the slab, board, or table, properly so called, was purposely not fastened or fixed to the frame-work or stand on which it was supported, but left loose, so as to be set on or taken off; and in 1555, on the accession of Queen Mary, when the stone altars were restored and the communion-tables taken down, we find it recorded of one John Austen, at Adesham Church, Kent, that "he with other tooke up the table, and laid it on a chest in the chancel, and set the tressels by it218-*."

It appears that texts of scripture were painted on the walls of some churches in the reign of Edward the Sixth; for Bonner, bishop of London, by a mandate issued to his diocese in 1554, after noticing that some had procured certain scriptures wrongly applied to be painted on church walls, charged that such scriptures should be razed, abolished, and extinguished, so that in no means they could be either read or heard.

In the articles set forth by Cardinal Pole in 1557, to be inquired of in his diocese of Canterbury, were the following: "Whether the churches be sufficiently garnished and adorned with all ornaments and books necessary; and whether they have a rood in their church of a decent stature, with Mary and John, and an image of the patron of the same church?" Also, "Whether the altars of the church be consecrated or no?"

But in 1559, the first year of the reign of Elizabeth, many of the injunctions set forth in the reign of Edward the Sixth, as to the mode of saying the Litany without procession, the removal and destruction of shrines and monuments of superstition, the setting up of a pulpit, and of the poor-box or chest, which latter was however "to be set and fastened in a most convenient place," were re-established. By these injunctions it appears that in many parts of the realm the altars of the churches had been removed, and tables placed for the administration of the holy sacrament; that in some other places the altars had not yet been removed: in the order whereof, as the injunctions express, save for an uniformity, there seemed to be no matter of great moment, so that the sacrament was duly and reverently ministered; and it was so ordered that no altar should be taken down but by oversight of the curate and churchwardens, or one of them, and that the holy table in every church should be decently made and set in the place where the altar stood, and there commonly covered, and so to stand, saving when the communion of the sacrament was to be distributed; at which time the same was to be so placed within the chancel in such manner that the minister might be the more conveniently heard of the communicants in his prayer and ministration.

Ancient Communion Table, Sunningwell Church, Berkshire.

Many of the old communion-tables set up in the reign of Elizabeth are yet remaining in our churches, and are sustained by a stand or frame, the bulging pillar-legs of which are often fantastically carved, with arabesque scroll-work and other detail according to the taste of the age. The communion-table in Sunningwell Church, Berkshire, probably set up during the time Bishop Jewell was pastor of that church, is a rich and interesting specimen. Communion-tables of the same era, designed in the same general style, with carved bulging legs, are preserved in the churches of Lapworth, Rowington, and Knowle, Warwickshire; in St. Thomas's Church, Oxford; and in many other churches. Sometimes the bulging pillar-legs are turned plain, and are not covered with carving: such occur in Broadwas Church, Worcestershire; in the churches of St. Nicholas and St. Helen, at Abingdon; and in the north aisle of Dorchester Church, Oxfordshire. The table or slab of the communion-table in Knowle Church is not fixed or fastened to the frame or stand on which it is placed, but lies loose; and this is also the case with an old communion-table of the sixteenth century, now disused, in Northleigh Church, Oxfordshire. In an inventory of church goods, taken in 1646, occurs the following: "Item, one *short table and frame*, commonly called the communion-table." On examining the old communion-tables, the movability of the slab from the frame-work is of such frequent occurrence as to corroborate the supposition that some esoteric meaning was attached to its unfixed state, which meaning has been attempted to be explained.

Under the colour of removing monuments of idolatry and false feigned images in the churches, much wanton spoliation and needless injury was effected; and this to such excess that in 1560 a royal proclamation was issued, commanding all persons to forbear the breaking or defacing of any monument or tomb, or any image of kings, princes, or nobles, or the breaking down and defacing of any image in glass windows, in any churches, without consent of the ordinary. And in the same year, in a letter from the queen to the commissioners for causes ecclesiastical, occasion is taken to remark that "in sundry churches and chappells where divine service, as prayer, preaching, and ministration of the sacraments be used, there is such negligence and lacke of convenient reverence used towardes the comelye keeping and order of the said churches, and especially of the upper parte called the chauncels, that it breedeth no small offence and slaunder to see and consider on the one part the curiositie and costes bestowed by all sortes of men upon there private houses, and the other part, the unclean or negligent order or sparekeeping of the house of prayer, by permitting open decaies, and ruines of coveringes, walls, and wyndowes, and by appointing unmeet and unseemly tables, with fowle clothes, for the communion of the sacraments, and generally leavynge the place of prayers desolate of all cleanlynes, and of meet ornaments for such a place, whereby it might be known a place provided for divine service." And the commissioners were required to consider the same, and in their discretion to determine upon some good and speedy means of reformation; and, amongst other things, to order that the tables of the commandments might be comely set or hung up in the east end of the chancel, to be not only read for edification, but also to give some comely ornament and demonstration that the same was a place of religion and prayer223-*.

An ancient table, apparently of this period, of the commandments painted on panel, but in language somewhat abbreviated, is still hung up against the east wall of the south transept of Ludlow Church, Salop224-*.

By the articles issued by royal authority in 1564, for administration of prayer and sacraments, each parish was to provide a decent table, standing on a frame, for the communion-table; this was to be decently covered with carpet, silk, or other decent covering, and with a fair linen cloth (at the time of the ministration); the ten commandments were to be set upon the east wall, over the table; the font was not to be removed, nor was the curate to baptize in parish churches in any basins.

In the Visitation Articles of Archbishop Parker, A. D. 1569, we find inquiries were to be made whether there was in each parish church a convenient pulpit well placed, a comely and decent table for the holy communion, covered decently and set in the place prescribed; and whether the altars had been taken down; also whether images and all other monuments of idolatry and superstition were destroyed and abolished; whether the rood-loft was pulled down, according to the order prescribed; and if the partition between the chancel and church was kept.

The latter inquiry is explanatory of the fact why, when the rood-lofts in many churches were taken down, the screens beneath them, separating the chancel from the nave, were left undisturbed.

By the injunctions of Grindal, archbishop of York, A. D. 1571, all altars were ordered to be pulled down to the ground, and the altar stones to be defaced and bestowed to some common use.

Pulpits of the reign of Edward the Sixth are rare, nor are those of the reign of Elizabeth very common. The pulpit in Fordington Church, Dorsetshire, of the latter period, is of stone, the upper part worked in plain oblong panels; and a kind of escutcheon within one of these bears the date 1592; the lower part or basement of this pulpit is circular in form.

The richly embroidered and costly vestments and antependia or frontals, of a period antecedent to the Reformation, were in some instances converted into coverings for the altar or communion table, or into hangings for the pulpit and reading desk. In Little Dean Church, Gloucestershire, the covering for the reading desk is formed out of an ancient sacerdotal vestment, probably a cope, of velvet, embroidered with portraits of saints. The cushion of the pulpit of East Langdon Church, near Dover, is made out of either an ancient antependium or vestment; the material consists of very thick crimson silk, embroidered with sprigs, and in the centre of the hanging are two figures supposed to represent the salutation of the Virgin, who is kneeling before a faldstool.

We occasionally, though rarely, meet with ancient charity-boxes of a date anterior to the Reformation: the churches of Wickmere, Loddon, and Causton, in Norfolk, still retain such226-*. At the Reformation, however, they were first required to be set up in churches. The ancient poor-box in Trinity Church, Coventry, is an excellent specimen of the Elizabethan era, and the shaft which supports it is of stone, covered with arabesque scroll-work and other detail peculiar to that age; but most of the old charity-boxes are of the seventeenth century.

Ancient Charity-box, Trinity Church, Coventry.

Towards the close of the sixteenth century the practice of preaching by an hour-glass, set in an iron frame affixed to the pulpit or projecting from the wall near it, began to prevail; and in the succeeding century this practice became quite common. In the churchwardens' accounts for St. Mary's Church, Lambeth, occurs the following: "A. 1579, Payde to Yorke for the frame on which the hower standeth,—..1..4;" and in the churchwardens' accounts of St. Helen's Church, Abingdon, is an item, "Anno MDXCI. payde for an houre glass for the pilpit, 4*d*." In the parochial accounts for St. Mary's, Shrewsbury, A. D. 1597, is a charge "for removing the desk and other necessaries about the pulpit, and for makeinge a thing for the hower glasse, 9*d*." In Shawell Church, Isle of Wight, the old iron stand for the hour-glass still remains affixed to a pier adjoining the pulpit; it is composed of two flat circular hoops or rings, one at some distance above the other, annexed or attached and kept in position by four vertical bars of iron, and the lower ring has cross-bars to sustain the glass. In Cassington Church, Oxfordshire, projecting from the wall by the side of the pulpit, is an iron stand for the hour-glass, consisting of two circular hoops or rings of iron, connected by four wrought iron bars, worked in the middle; and across the lower ring or hoop is an iron bar or stay. In High Laver Church, Essex, the iron stand for the glass still remains, and is in fashion not unlike a cresset, having only one hoop or ring encircling the top, and supported on four iron bars, which cross in curves at the bottom. Many other churches might be enumerated in which the stand for the hour-glass is still preserved; and the hour-glass itself, together with its frame, is said to be retained in South Burlingham Church, Norfolk. An hour-glass within a rich and peculiar frame, supported on a spiral column, and apparently of the latter part of the seventeenth century, is yet preserved in St. Alban's Church, Wood Street, London.

Hour-glass Frame, Shawell Church, Isle of Wight.

To the close of the sixteenth century the mode of pewing with open low-backed seats continued to prevail; the ends of these seats were not covered with tracery or arched panel-work, but were plain, though they sometimes terminated with a finial. In the nave of Stanton St. John Church, Oxfordshire, are some old open pews or seats, apparently of the reign of Henry the Eighth, the backs of which are divided diamond-wise, and form a kind of lattice-work, and the ends terminate in grotesque heads. In Harrington Church, Worcestershire, are some open seats of plain workmanship, bearing the date of 1582. The church of Sunningwell, Berkshire, is fitted up with a range of open seats on each side of the nave, without any ornament, with the exception of a large carved finial at the end of each seat. In Cowley Church, near Oxford, are open seats of the date of

1632, which have at the ends finials carved in the shallow angular designs of that period. All these seats are appropriately placed, or disposed facing the east, and none are turned with the backs towards the altar230-*. About the commencement of the seventeenth century our churches began to be disfigured by the introduction of high pews, an innovation which did not escape censure; for, as Weaver observes, "Many monuments of the dead in churches in and about this citie of London, as also in some places in the countrey, are covered with seates or pewes, made high and easie for the parishioners to sit or sleepe in; a fashion of no long continuance, and worthy of reformation231-*." The high pews set up in the early part of this century are easily distinguished by the flat and shallow carved scroll and arabesque work with which the sides and doors are covered. In the directions given on the primary visitation of Wren, bishop of Norwich, A. D. 1636, we find an order "that the chancels and alleys in the church be not encroached upon by building of seats; and if any be so built, the same to be removed and taken away; and that no pews be made over high, so that they which be in them cannot be seen how they behave themselves, or the prospect of the church or chancel be hindered; and therefore that all pews which within do much exceed a yard in height be taken down near to that scantling, unless the bishop by his own inspection, or by the view of some special commissioner, shall otherwise allow."

From a paper found among secretary Cecil's MSS.232-*, it appears that in 1564 some ministers performed divine service and prayers in the chancel, others in the body of the church, and some *in a seat made in the church*; and in the parochial accounts of St. Mary's Church, Shrewsbury, A. D. 1577, is an entry "for coloringe the curate's pew and dask;" but no public notice of the modern reading desk, or, as it was called, the "reading pew," occurs till 1603, when, in the ecclesiastical canons then framed, it was enjoined that besides the pulpit a fitting or convenient seat should be constructed for the minister to read service in; and in allusion to the reading desk, Bishop Sparrow, in his Rationale of the Book of Common Prayer, observes, "This was the ancient custom of the church of England, that the priest who did officiate in all those parts of the service which were directed to the people turned himself towards them, as in the absolution; but in those parts of the office which were directed to God immediately, as prayers, hymns, lauds, confessions of faith or sins, he turned from the people; and for that purpose, in many parish churches of late, the reading pew had one desk for the Bible, looking towards the people to the body of the church, another for the prayer-book, looking towards the east or upper end of the chancel. And very reasonable was this usage; for when the people was spoken to it was fit to look towards them, but when God was spoken to it was fit to turn from the people." And so he goes on to explain the custom of turning to the east in public prayer.

In Bishop Wren's directions it was enjoined that the minister's reading desk should not stand with the back towards the chancel, nor too remote or far from it.

The double reading desk is still occasionally met with, as in East Ilsley Church, Berkshire, where is a kind of double reading desk so that the minister can turn himself either towards the west or south. In Priors Salford Church, Warwickshire, is an old carved reading pew bearing the date of its construction, 1616; and in St. Peter's Church, Dorchester, Dorsetshire, and in Sherbourne Church, in the same county, are reading pews which evidently, from the style and the carved work with which they are covered, were constructed in the early part of the seventeenth century.

The enclosing of the communion table in the church of Stow, in the county of Norfolk, by rails, about the year 1622, is noticed by Weaver, who states that the vicar and churchwardens pulled down a tomb to make room for the rail.

In Bishop Wren's diocesan directions it was ordered that the communion table in every church should always stand close under the east wall of the chancel, the ends thereof north and south, and that the rail should be made before it, reaching up from the north wall to the south wall, near one yard in height, so thick with pillars that dogs might not get in.

But we find the situation of the altar or communion table, and the reason of its severance by means of rails, more particularly noticed in the canons entertained by the convocation held in 1640. In these (after an allusion to the fact that many had been misled against the rites and ceremonies of the church of England, and had taken offence at the same upon an unjust supposal that they were introductive unto popish superstitions, whereas they had been duly and ordinarily practised by the whole church during a great part of the reign of Queen Elizabeth, and that though since that time they had by subtle practices begun to fall into disuse, and in place thereof other foreign and unfitting usages by little and little to creep in, yet in the royal chapels and many other churches most of them had been ever constantly used and observed) it was declared that the standing of the communion table sideway under the east window of every chancel was in its own nature indifferent235-*; yet as it had been ordered by the injunctions of Queen Elizabeth that the holy tables should stand in the places where the altars stood, it was judged fit and convenient that all churches should conform themselves in this particular to the example of the cathedral and mother churches; and it was declared that this situation of the holy table did not imply that it was or ought to be esteemed a true and proper altar, whereon Christ was again really sacrificed; but that it was and might be called an altar, in that sense in which the primitive church called it an altar, and in no other. And because experience had shewn how irreverent the behaviour of many people was in many places, (some leaning, others casting their hats, and some sitting upon, some standing, and others sitting under the communion table, in time of divine service,) for the avoiding of which and like abuses it was thought meet and convenient that the communion tables in all churches should be decently severed with rails, to preserve them from such or worse profanations.

Communion rails carved in the nondescript style, almost peculiar to the reign of Charles the First, are preserved in St. Giles's Church, Oxford; in the Lady Chapel, Winchester Cathedral; in the Church of St. Cross, near Winchester; in the choir of Worcester Cathedral; and in Andover Church, Hants: in which last instance the rails are composed of open semicircular arches, supported on baluster columns, with pendants similar to hip knobs hanging from the arches; but specimens of altar rails of a period antecedent to the Restoration are not often to be met with, the reason for which will be adduced.

By the canons of 1603 the churchwardens or questmen were to provide in every church a comely and decent pulpit, to be set in a convenient place within the same, and there to be seemly kept for the preaching of God's word. Carved pulpits set up between the years 1603 and 1640 are numerous, and the sides are more or less embellished with circular-arched panels, flat and shallow scroll-work, and other decorative detail in fashion at that period; and not a few bear the precise date of their construction.

In the nave of Bristol Cathedral is a stone pulpit, ascended to by means of a circular flight of steps; the sides are panelled and ornamented with escutcheons surrounded by scroll-work, and it bears the date of 1624.

In Ashington Church, Somersetshire, is a pulpit with the date 1627.

In Bradford Abbas Church, Dorsetshire, is a fine carved wooden pulpit and sounding-board, and on it appears the date 1632.

The date of 1625 appears on a fine carved wooden pulpit, the sides of which are covered with semicircular-headed panels, in Huish Episcopi Church, Somersetshire.

In one of the churches at Wells is a fine wooden pulpit, of the date 1636; at the angles are columns of semi-classic design, fantastically carved; the panels are curiously ornamented with figures in relief, and it is supported on a stand composed of a square and four detached columns, above which are represented a number of birds with large beaks; the sounding-board over corresponds in design with the pulpit.

A very fine carved wooden pulpit, the sides of which are embellished with circular-arched panel and scroll-work, with the date 1640, and a sounding-board over, is contained in Cerne Abbas Church, Dorsetshire.

Many carved pulpits of this era have, however, no assigned date; they are commonly placed at the north or south-east angle of the nave, but never in the middle of the aisle, so as to obstruct the view of the communion table.

The commandments were again, by the canons of 1603, ordered to be set upon the east end of every church, where the people might best see and read the same; and other chosen sentences were to be written upon the walls of the churches in places convenient.

On the south wall of Rowington Church, Warwickshire, are sentences painted with a border of scroll-work; the like also occur at Astley Church, in the same county; and on the walls of Bradford Abbas Church, Dorsetshire, are sentences of scripture painted in black-lettered characters within panels surrounded by scroll-work.

By the same canons the churchwardens were required to provide, if such had not been already provided, a strong chest, with a hole in the upper part thereof, having three keys, of which one was to remain in the custody of the minister, and the other two in the custody of the churchwardens; which chest was to be set and fastened in the most convenient place, to the intent the parishioners might put into it their alms for their poor neighbours.

In the retro-choir, Sherbourne Church, Dorsetshire, is a poor-box with three locks; and a carved poor-box, of the early part of the seventeenth century, is preserved in Harlow Church, Essex. In Elstow Church, Bedfordshire, are the remains of a poor-box of the same period. In Clapham Church, in the same county, is an old poor-box, the cover of which is gone, on which are the initials I. W., and the date 1626: this is fixed on a plain wooden pillar near the south door; and in the south aisle of Bletchley Church, Buckinghamshire, is an oak pillar or shaft surmounted by a poor-box, with an inscription carved on it of "Remember the Pore," and the date 1637240-*.

The communion tables of the early part of this century were not so richly carved as those of the reign of Elizabeth, and in general the pillar-legs were plain and not so bulging; but the frieze or upper part of the frame-work, on which the table rested, was often covered with shallow and flat carved panel and scroll-work, and sometimes with the date of its construction.

In the church of St. Lawrence, at Evesham, the communion table bears the date of 1610; and round the frieze is carved an inscription, stating by whom it was given. In Cerne Abbas Church, Dorsetshire, is a carved communion table, bearing the date of 1638. The communion table in Godshill Church, Isle of Wight, is supported on four carved bulging pillar-legs; and round the frieze, below the ledge of the table, is the following inscription:

"Lancelot Coleman & Edward Britwel, Churchwardens, Anno Dom. 1631."

In Whitwell Church, Isle of Wight, the communion table stands on plain bulging pillar-legs; and on the frieze round the ledge is carved in relief an arm holding a chalice, with the following inscription:

"I will take the cup of salvation, and call upon the name of the Lord. Psa. 116. v. 53. Anno Dom. 1632."

As the rubric of the church enjoined that at the communion the priest should himself place the elements upon the holy table, the custom of having a side table, called the credence table, for the elements to be set on previous to their removal by the priest to the communion table for consecration, was observed in some churches in the latter part of the sixteenth and early part of the seventeenth century. Such table appears to have been introduced in the reign of Elizabeth, by Andrews, bishop of Norwich, whose model Archbishop Laud is said to have followed242-*; and it originated from the πρόθεσις, or side table of preparation, used in the early church; it was likewise, as we have seen, used at the sacramentals of the church of Rome, and on that account was strongly objected to by the Puritans.

Table, (temp. Charles I.,) Chipping-Warden Church, Northamptonshire.

In the chancel of Chipping-Warden Church, Northamptonshire, on the north side of the communion table, is a semicircular oak table, apparently of the reign of Charles the First, standing on a frame supported by three plain pillar-legs, like those of the communion tables of the same period, and enriched with carved arched frieze-work similar to the arched panel-work on pulpits of the same period.

A plain credence table of black oak, which from the style and make was evidently set up after the Restoration, still continues to be used as such in St. Michael's Church, Oxford, being placed on the north side of the communion table.

The objections of the Puritans against many of the usages of the Anglican church, and their refusal to conform to such under the pretence of their being superstitious, had no slight effect in altering the internal appearance of our churches in the middle of the seventeenth century, and during the period their party had obtained the ascendancy, and had succeeded for a while in abolishing in this country episcopal church government; for among the "innovations in discipline," as they were called by the Puritan committee of the House of Lords in 1641, we find the following usages complained of: the turning of the holy table altarwise, and most commonly calling it an altar; the bowing towards it or towards the east many times; advancing candlesticks in many churches upon the altar, so called; the making of canopies over the altar, so called, with traverses and curtains on each side and before it; the compelling all communicants to come up to the rails, and there to receive; the advancing crucifixes and images upon the parafront or altar cloth, so called; the reading some part of the morning prayer at the holy table, when there was no communion celebrated; the minister's turning his back to the west, and his face to the east, when he pronounced the Creed or read prayers; the reading the Litany in the midst of the body of the church in many of the parochial churches; the having a *credentia* or side table, besides the Lord's table, for divers uses in the Lord's Supper; and the taking down galleries in churches, or restraining the building of galleries where the parishes were very populous244-*.

In August, 1643, an Ordinance of the Lords and Commons was published, for the taking away and demolishing of all altars and tables of stone, and for the removal of all communion tables from the east end of every church and chancel; and it was prescribed that such should be placed in some other fit and convenient place in the body of the church or in the body of the chancel; and that all rails whatsoever which had been erected near to, before, or about any altar or communion table, should be likewise taken away; and that the chancel-ground which had been raised within twenty years then last past, for any altar or communion table to stand on, should be laid down and levelled, as the same had formerly been; and that all tapers, candlesticks, and basins should be removed and taken away from the communion table, and not again used about the same; and that all crucifixes, crosses, and all images and pictures of any one or more Persons of the Trinity, or of the Virgin Mary, and all other images and pictures of saints, or superstitious inscriptions belonging to any churches, should be taken away and defaced before the first day of November, 1643: but it was provided that such ordinances should not extend to any image, picture, or coat of arms, in glass, stone, or otherwise, set up or graven only for a monument of any dead person not reputed for a saint, but that all such might stand and continue.

By a subsequent ordinance, passed in May, 1644, it was prescribed that no rood-loft or holy water fonts should be any more used in any church; and that all organs, and the frames or cases in which they stood, in all churches, should be taken away and utterly defaced.

Under colour of these ordinances the beauty of the cathedrals and churches was injured to an extent hardly credible; the monuments of the dead were defaced, and brasses torn away, in the iconoclastic fury which then raged; the very tombs were violated; and the havoc made of church ornaments, and destruction of the fine painted glass with which most church windows then abounded, may in some degree be estimated from the account given by one Dowsing, a parliamentary visitor appointed under a warrant from the Earl of Manchester for demolishing the so called superstitious pictures and ornaments of churches within the county of Suffolk, who kept a journal, with the particulars of his transactions, in the years 1643 and 1644: these were chiefly comprised in the demolition of numerous windows filled with painted glass, in the breaking down of altar rails and organ cases, in levelling the steps in the chancels, in removing crucifixes, in taking down the stone crosses from the exterior of the churches, in defacing crosses on the fonts, and in the taking up (under the pretence of their being superstitious) of numerous sepulchral inscriptions in brass. Nor did the churches in other parts of the country, with some exceptions, escape from a like fanatical warfare; and, in this, many of our cathedrals suffered most. But this was not enough: our sacred edifices were profaned and polluted in the most irreverent and disgraceful manner; and with the exception of the destruction which took place on the dissolution of the monastic establishments in the previous century, more devastation was committed at this time by the party hostile to the Anglican church than had ever before been effected since the ravages of the ancient Danish invaders.

But as to other alterations at this time effected. In January, 1644, an ordinance of parliament was published for the taking away of the Book of Common Prayer, which was forbid to be used any longer in any church, chapel, or place of public worship. In lieu of this the "Directory for the Publike Worship of God" was established: this contained no stated forms of prayer, but general instructions only for extemporaneous praying and preaching, and for the administration of the sacraments of Baptism and the Lord's Supper; the former of which was to be administered in the place of public worship and in the face of the congregation, but "not," as the Directory expresses, "in the places where fonts in the time of popery were unfitly and superstitiously placed." And at the administration of the Lord's Supper the table was to be so placed that the communicants might sit orderly about it or at it; but all liturgical form was abolished, and the prayers even at this sacrament were such as the minister might spontaneously offer.

At Brill Church, in Buckinghamshire, the communion table, on an elevation of one step, is inclosed with rails, within an area of eight feet by six feet and a half, and a bench is fixed to the wall on each side; an innovation made at this period, in order that the communicants might receive the sacrament sitting. The communion table in Wooten Wawen Church, Warwickshire, though perfectly plain in construction, is unusually long and large, and appears to have been set up by the Puritans at this period, so that they might sit round or at it.

To the removal of the communion table from the east end of the chancel may be attributed the usage which, in the middle of the seventeenth century, began to prevail of constructing close and high seats or pews, without regard to that uniformity of arrangement which had hitherto been observed; and many seats were now so constructed that those who occupied them necessarily turned their backs on the east during the ministration of prayer and public service. The erection of unseemly galleries, which have greatly tended to disfigure our churches, was another consequence of the innovation on the ancient arrangement of pewing.

After the Restoration the communion tables were again restored to their former position at the east end of the chancel; and in Evelyn's Diary for 1661-2, we find the change of position in his parish church thus noticed: "6 April. Being of the vestry in the afternoone, we order'd that the communion table should be set as usual altarwise, with a decent raile in front, as before the rebellion."

The altar rails were now generally restored, and in most instances we find those in our churches to be of a period subsequent to the Restoration, as the details in the workmanship evince. In the church accounts of St.

Mary's, Shrewsbury, for 1662, we find a "memorandum that this year the rayles about the communion table wer new sett up, and the surplice was made." In Wormleighton Church, Warwickshire, the altar rails have on them the date of 1664; and the communion table, which is quite plain, is of the same character and era.

But a return, after the Restoration, to the former usages of the Anglican church was not made without great opposition; and accordingly we find objections stated to the bowing to the altar and to the east, to the preaching by book, to the railing in of the altar, to the candles, cushion, and book thereon, to the bowing at the name of Jesus, and to the organs as "popish-like music, and too much superstition250-*."

When the rood was taken down at the Reformation, a custom began to prevail of fixing up in its stead or place, against the arch leading into the chancel, the upper part of which was in consequence blocked up by it, and facing the congregation, so as to be seen by them, the royal arms, with proper heraldic supporters; but it does not clearly appear that this was done in consequence of any express law or injunction to that effect, though it may perhaps have served to denote the king's supremacy. We seldom, however, find the royal arms of earlier date than the Restoration, in the twenty years previous to which they appear to have been generally taken down. In Brixton Church, Isle of Wight, on some plain wooden panelling between the tower and a gallery at the west end are the remains of the royal arms, which, from the style in which they have been painted with the rose and thistle, appear coeval with the reign of James the First; they are surmounted by a crown, below which is an open six-barred helme. These arms appear to have been removed from their original position against the chancel-arch, and are now much mutilated. In the church accounts, St. Mary's, Shrewsbury, for 1651, is a charge of 1*l.* 8*s.* "for making the states armes." In Anstey Church, Warwickshire, the arms of the commonwealth, put up during the inter-regnum, were taken down not many years back. The little church of St. Lawrence, in the Isle of Wight, still retains the royal arms put up at the Restoration in 1660.

Excepting the rood-loft galleries, we have few galleries in our churches of a period antecedent to the latter part of the seventeenth century. At the west end of Worstead Church, Norfolk, over the west door, is a gallery erected in 1550, at the cost of the candle called the Bachelor's Light. At the west end of the nave in Leighton Buzzard Church is a gallery erected in 1634; and at the west end of Piddletown Church, Dorsetshire, is a gallery with the date of its erection, 1635.

From about the period of the Revolution, in 1688, we may trace the commencement of a custom, still partially prevailing, of setting up the pulpit and reading-pew in the middle aisle, in front of the communion table; so that during the whole of the service the back of the minister was turned to the east, and the view of the communion table obstructed; but we have not found any pulpit thus placed of an earlier period.

We still retain, in the Anglican church, the usage of placing two candlesticks and candles upon the communion table, in compliance with the injunctions of King Edward the Sixth, together also with an offertory dish; of reading the lessons from the eagle desk, and of saying the Litany at the litany-stool. These practices are, however, more particularly observed in our cathedrals and college chapels than in our parochial churches, in most of which they have fallen into desuetude.

To conclude, in the language of the synod held in 1640: "Whereas the church is the house of God, dedicated to his holy worship, and therefore ought to remind us both of the greatness and goodness of his Divine Majesty; certain it is that the acknowledgment thereof, not only inwardly in our hearts, but also outwardly with our bodies, must needs be pious in itself, profitable unto us, and edifying unto others: we therefore think it meet and behoveful, and heartily commend it to all good and well-affected people, members of this church, that they be ready to tender unto the Lord the said acknowledgment, by doing reverence and obeisance, both at their coming in and going out of the said churches, chancels, or chapels, according to the most ancient custom of the primitive church in the purest times, and of this church also for many years of the reign of Queen Elizabeth.

"The reviving, therefore, of this ancient and laudable custom we heartily recommend to the serious consideration of all good people, not with any intention to exhibit any religious worship to the communion table, the east, or church, or any thing therein contained, in so doing; or to perform the said gesture in the celebration of the holy eucharist, upon any opinion of a corporal presence of the body of Jesus Christ on the holy table or in the mystical elements, but only for the advancement of God's majesty, and to give him alone that honour and glory that is due unto him, and no otherwise; and in the practice or omission of this rite we desire that the rule of charity prescribed by the apostle may be observed, which is, that they which use this rite despise not them who use it not, and that they who use it not condemn not those that use it."

"... a bloodie crosse he bore,
The deare remembrance of his dying Lord,
For whose sweete sake that glorious badge he wore,
And dead, as living, ever him ador'd:
Upon his shield the like was also scor'd."

154-* Hist. Eccles. lib. vi. c. 6. Durantus, however, assigns a different origin. "In veteri testamento non nisi lotus templum ingrediebatur." De Labro, seu Vase Aquæ Benedictæ, c. 21.

156-* "Ad valvas ecclesiæ,"—Ordo ad Faciendum Catechumenum, Manuale.

156-† Constitutions of Edmund Archbishop of Canterbury, A. D. 1236. De Baptismo et eius Effectu."

158-* It is much to be regretted that of late years many ancient fonts have been cast out of our churches, and earthenware and pewter basins substituted in their stead for the administration of the holy sacrament of baptism: a practice not authorized by the Anglican church, but rather condemned; for in the canons set forth by authority, A. D. 1571, it is provided that "Curabunt (Œditui) ut in singulis ecclesiis sit sacer fons, *non pelvis*, in quo baptismus ministretur, isque ut decenter et munde conservetur." And in the canons of 1603, after alluding to the foregoing constitution, and observing that it was too much neglected in many places, it is appointed "That there shall be a font of stone in every church and chapel where baptism is to be ministered; the same to be set in the *ancient usual places.*" In the orders and directions given by Bishop Wren, A. D.

1636, to be observed in his diocese of Norwich, we find it enjoined, "That the font at baptism be filled with clear water, and no dishes, pails, or basins be used in it or instead of it."

160-* The 28th decree of a foreign council, that of Wirtzburgh, held A. D. 1278, prohibits the fortifying of churches in order to make use of them as castles.

164-* Anglice sermocinari solebat (Abbas Samson) populo, sed secundum Linguam Norfolchie ... unde et pulpitum jussit fieri in ecclesia et ad utilitatem audiencium et ad decorem ecclesie.—Cronica Jocelini de Brakelonda, sub anno 1187.

167-* Cottonian MS. Titus D. xxvii. 10th sæc.

167-† "Crux que erat super magnum altare, et Mariola, et Johannes, quas imagines Stigandus archiepiscopus magno pondere auri et argenti ornaverat, et sancto Ædmundo dederat."—Cronica Jocelini de Brakelonda, p. 4.

168-* "Supra pulpitum trabes erat, per tranversum ecclesiæ posita, quæ crucem grandem et duo cherubin et imagines Sanctæ *Mariæ* et Sancti *Johannis* apostoli sustentabat."—Gervasius de Combustione, &c.

169-* "Superest exponere, quod manus illa e nubibus erumpens indicet: Quæ procul dubio omnipotentis Dei dexteram designat."—Ciampini Vetera Monimenta, vol. ii. pp. 22, 81.

171-* "In elevatione atque utriusque squilla pulsatur."—Durandi Rationale, lib. iv.

171-† In Yeovil Church Accounts, A. D. 1457, is an item, "*In una cordul empt p le salsyngbelle ijd.*"—Collectanea Topographica, vol. iii. p. 130.

172-* It is now in the possession of William Staunton, esq., of Longbridge House, near Warwick.

173-* Durandus, in his description of a church, makes no mention of screen-work, but observes, "Notandum est quod triplex genus *veli* suspenditur in ecclesia videlicet quod sacra operit, quod sanctuarium a clero dividit, *et quod clerum a populo secernit*;" evidently alluding in the latter to the curtain extended across the chancel arch.

174-* "Item tunc stent in sedibus suis versa facie ad altare donec ad *misericordias* vel super *formulas* prout tempus postulat inclinent."—Monasticon, 1st ed. vol. i. p. 951.

180-* The placing of more than two lights on the altar seems never to have been practised in the churches of this country; at least I have not met with any ancient illumination in which more than two are represented.

181-* The cover of an ancient thurible of latten was lately discovered in the chest of Ashbury Church, Berkshire: the lower part is of a semi-globular or domical form, from which issues an embattled turret or lantern in the form of a pentagon, which is finished by a quadrangular spire; the sides both of the lantern and spire are partly of open work, and round the domical part is inscribed *Gloria Tibi Domine*.

181-† A small ampulla of brass or latten, supposed to have been an ancient chrismatory for the consecrated oil used in the sacrament of extreme unction, has been within the last few years discovered in the castle ditch, Pulford, Cheshire: this curious little relic is not more than two inches high; the body is semi-globular, or bulges in front, with a plain Greek cross engraved on it, and is flattened at the back; and at the neck are two bowed handles, by chains attached to which it appears to have hung suspended from the shoulders.

182-* Harding, in his controversy with Bishop Jewell, mentions "the monstrance or pixe" as if one and the same article.—Defence of the Apology, &c., p. 343.

183-* Quo finito sacerdos cum suis ministris in sedibus ad hos paratis se recipiant et expectent usque ad orationem dicendam vel alio tempore usque ad *Gloria in excelsis*.—MS. Rituale pen. Auc.

183-† This arrangement was different to that directed by the rubrical orders of the Roman missals, on their revision after the council of Trent, by which the celebrant was to be seated between the deacon and sub-deacon: "In missa item solemni celebrans medius inter diaconum et sub-diaconum sedere potest a cornu epistolæ juxta altare cum cantatur *Kyrie eleison, Gloria in excelsis*, et *Credo*."—Missale Romanum, Antverpiæ, MDCXXXI.; Rubricæ Generales, &c. One of the queries published by Le Brun, whilst composing his liturgical work, was, "Si le prêtre s'assied au dessus du diacre et du soudiacre, ou au milieu d'eux."

186-* Prope altare collocatur Piscina seu Lavacrum in quo manus lavantur.—Durandi Rat. de Ecclesia, &c. In ancient church contracts the term *Lavatorie* was sometimes used for the Piscina, as in that for Catterick Church. In the Roman Missal subsequent to the Tridentine council the word *Sacrarium* is used.

187-* At Alvechurch, Worcestershire, the custom prevails of the priest washing his hands in the vestry before the administration of the sacrament, and napkins are brought to dry his hands.

189-* "Il y avoit pour cet effet en chaque piscine, comme en peut voir encore à une infinité d'autels, deux conduits, ou canaux, pour faire écouler l'eau, l'un pour recevoir l'eau qui avoit servi au lavement des mains, l'autre pour celle qui avoit servi au purification ou perfusion du chalice."—De Vert, Explication des Cérémonies de l'Eglise, vol. iii. p. 193.

190-* In "Le Parfaict Ecclesiastique, par M. Claude de la Croix," (a curious work published A. D. 1666, and containing full instructions for the clergy of the Gallican church, and an exposition of the rites and ceremonies,) amongst appendages to an altar is enumerated "une credance ou niche dans le mur a poser les burettes et le bassin," p. 536. And in another place, "au costé de l'Autel il y faut une petite niche à poser les burettes et le bassin, et y faire un trou en facon de piscine a fin que l'eau se perde en terre." p. 568.

190-† "In cornu Epistolæ ... ampullæ vitreæ vini et aquæ cum pelvicula et manutergio mundo in fenestella seu in parva mensa ad hæc praeparata"—Missale Romanum ex Decreto, &c. 1631.

"Calix vero et alia necessaria praeparentur in credentia cooperta linteo, antequam sacerdos veniat ad altare."—Ibid.

192-* The earliest account of the sepulchre thus set up that I have yet met with occurs in an inventory of church furniture, A. D. 1214, in which is mentioned *"velum unum de serico supra sepulchrum."*

193-* "Table" was a word used to express any sculptured basso relievo, more especially that inserted in the wall over an altar.

199-* A series of coloured engravings from the paintings on the walls of this chapel, which were evidently executed at the close of the fifteenth century, was published in 1807 by the late Mr. Thomas Fisher.

200-* By an injunction set forth by royal authority, A. D. 1539, it was ordered, "That from henceforth the said Thomas Becket shall not be esteemed, named, reputed, and called a saint, but Bishop Becket; and that his images and pictures thorow the whole realme shal be pluckt downe and avoided out of all churches, chapel, and other places."—Fox's Martyrology.

209-* The locality, character, and construction of the confessional in our ancient churches are not yet clearly elucidated. Du Cange described the confessional, *"confessio,"* simply as "cellula in qua presbyteri fidelium confessiones excipiebant;" whilst according to De la Croix, in his remarks on those of the Gallican churches in the middle of the seventeenth century, "Les confessionaux doiuent estre à l'entrée des Eglises, et non pas auprés des Autels, ny dans le Chœur, ny en lieu caché, et tousieurs vne ouuerture pour écouter le Penitent, avec vn treillis de bois ou autre estoffe, et vn volet pour le fermer, quand on écoute de l'vn des costez ouuert."

210-* The tabard or heraldic coat worn over the body armour, and still worn by the heralds on state occasions.

211-* "Our churches stand full of such great puppets, wondrously decked and adorned; garlands and coronets be set on their heads, precious pearls hanging about their necks; their fingers shine with rings set with precious stones; their dead and stiff bodies are clothed with garments stiff with gold."—Homily against Peril of Idolatry.

215-* In the injunctions given by Bishop Ridley, in the visitation of his diocese A. D. 1550, occurs the following: "Item that the minister in the time of the communion, immediately after the offertory, shall monish the communicants, saying these words, or such like, 'Now is the time, if it please you, to remember the poor men's chest with your charitable alms.'"

216-* Dr. Cardwell, in his editorial preface to the reprint of the two Books of Common Prayer set forth in the reign of Edward the Sixth, observes, "The communion service of the first liturgy contained a prayer for the descent of the Holy Spirit upon the bread and wine, and a following prayer of oblation, which, together with the form of words addressed to the communicants, were designed to represent a sacrifice, and appeared to undiscriminating minds to denote the sacrifice of the mass. Numerous, therefore, and urgent were the objections against this portion of the service. Combined with a large class of objectors, whose theology consisted merely in an undefined dread of Romanism, were all those, however differing among themselves, who believed the holy communion to be a feast and not a sacrifice, and that larger class of persons who, placing the solemn duty upon its proper religious basis, were contented to worship without waiting to refine."

218-* Fox's Martyrology.

223-* In compliance with the queen's letter, the following directions were sent by the commissioners to the dean and chapter of Bristol:

"After our hartie comendacōns.—Whereas we are credibly informed that there are divers tabernacles for Images, as well in the fronture of the roodeloft of the cath^l church of Bristol, as also in the frontures, back, and ends of the walles wheare the comñ table standeth, for asmoch as the same churche shoulde be a light and good example to th' ole citie and dioc. we have thought good to direct these our lrēs unto you, and to require youe to cause the said tabernacles to be defaced & hewen downe, and afterwards to be made a playne walle, wth morter, plast^r, or otherways, & some scriptures to be written in the places, & namely that upon the walle on the east end of the quier wheare the comn table usually doth stande, the table of the comand[ts] to be painted in large caracters, with convenient speed, and furniture according to the orders latly set furthe by vertue of the quenes ma[ts] comission for causes ecclesiasticall, at the coste and chardges of the said churche; whereof we require you not to faile. And so we bed you farewell. From London, the xxi. of December, 1561."—Britton's Bristol Cath. p. 52.

224-* In the chancel of Bengeworth Church, Gloucestershire, is a table of the commandments, with the letters cut in box-wood. This has the date of 1591 upon it.

226-* These are engraved in vol. xx. of the Archæologia, and, from the general style and mouldings, appear to have been constructed in the latter part of the fifteenth century.

230-* The symbolical turning towards the east whilst pronouncing the Creed is adverted to by St. Cyril. In the Apostolical Constitutions, book ii. sect. xxviii., the attendants at public worship are enjoined to pray to God eastward. The custom of turning to the east at prayer is noticed by many of the early fathers of the church, and among them by St. Basil, who remarks, "As to the doctrines and preachings which are preserved in the church, we have some of them from the written doctrine; others we have received as delivered from the tradition of the apostles in a mystery. For, to begin with the mention of what is first and most common, who has taught us by writing that those that hope in the name of our Lord should be signed with the sign of the cross? what written law has taught us that we should turn towards the east in our prayers?.... Is not all this derived from this concealed and mystical tradition?.... We all, indeed, look towards the east in our prayers."—Basil, Epist. ad Amphiloc. de Spiritu S. Whiston's translation in Essay on the Apostolical Constitutions.

231-* Funeral Monuments, A. D. 1631, p. 701.

232-* Printed in Strype's Life of Parker. In the same paper the communion table is noticed as standing in the body of the church in some places, in others standing in the chancel; in some places standing altarwise, distant from the wall a yard, in others in the middle of the chancel, north and south; in some places *the table was joined, in others it stood upon tressels*; in some the table had a carpet, in others none.

235-* "The position of the table had now become the token of a distinct and solemn belief as to the nature of the eucharist, and was therefore treated as a question of conscience and an article of faith."—Cardwell's Documentary Annals, vol. ii. p. 186, note. The extracts given from the injunctions have been principally taken from this work.

240-* The unostentatious and laudable practice of bestowing alms to the charity-box has long fallen into disuse in most churches; but within the last few years charity-boxes have been set up in some of our churches, and this commendable custom is again gradually reviving.

242-* Neal's History of the Puritans, vol. iii. p. 170.

244-* Cardwell's Conferences, p. 272.

250-* Hickeringill's Ceremony-Monger, (pub. 1689,) p. 63.